Laleh Bakhtiar

SUFI

Expressions of the Mystic Quest

Thames and Hudson

Art and Imagination
General Editor: Jill Purce

Printed in Singapore

Contents

TO HELEN

Note: the letter ص which follows the name of the Prophet Muḥammad (ص) is a customary abbreviation for the benediction *salli ʿaLāh ʿalīh wa ālihī*, ('may the blessings of God be upon him and his family').

Part 1
The 'Why' of Mystical Expression

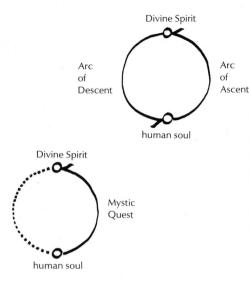

The Sufi, through creative expression, remembers and invokes the Divine order as It resides in a hidden state within all forms. To remember and to invoke, in this sense, are the same: to act on a form so that that which is within may become known. The Sufi thus re-enacts the process of creation whereby the Divine came to know Itself. The receptacle in which the creation is re-enacted may be an external form such as an artifact, or it may be the life form of the mystic which is transformed. Here the very soul of the Sufi-to-be reaches towards the Divine centre through the mystic Quest.

THE BEGINNINGS OF SUFISM

According to the followers of the Sufi path, Sufism in its essence is timeless; but its historical manifestation begins with the descent of the Quran (p. 52). Some sources trace the origin to an incident that occurred to the Prophet Muḥammad (ﷺ). One day, while he was teaching the verse, 'God created the seven heavens' (65:12), a special meaning of this verse was revealed to him. Ibn ʿAbbas, the great transmitter of his Traditions, who was present, was later asked what the Prophet had said. Ibn ʿAbbas answered, 'If I were to tell you, you would stone me to death.' Through this allusion to the inner meaning of things, the meaning which is not comprehensible to all, the inner path to God was opened (p. 38). The Companions of the Prophet were devout men who performed acts of meditation and constant remembrance of the Divine through Its Names and through repetition of the text of the Quran; and after the death of the Prophet this group spread and trained disciples. The name of Sufi was still unknown.

At the beginning of the eighth century AD (2nd Islamic century), these ascetics came to be known as Sufis. The derivation of this word is not known for certain. It may come from the word meaning 'wool', referring to the rough woollen garments they wore; it may come from the word meaning 'purity'. Some say the word stems from 'line', referring to the people who prayed in a line directly behind the Prophet. Still others among the Sufis themselves say the word is too sublime to be derived from anything.

In another Tradition of the Prophet, his Ascent or Night Journey (p. 85) is described in part in the following manner:

'On my spiritual ascent I was taken to Paradise. I was placed before the door of a house. Gabriel was at the door. I asked to be let in. Gabriel said, "I am only a servant of God. You must pray to God if you want the door to be opened," and so I did. God said, "I open the door only to those who are most beloved. You and your followers are most dear," and the door was opened. Inside I saw a casket made of white pearls. I asked Gabriel to open the box. He told me only God could do so. I asked it of God, and the box was opened. God said, "That which the box contains will be held for you and your progeny." The box contained two things: spiritual poverty and a cloak. When I descended, I brought the cloak with me and I put it on ʿAlī's shoulders, and after ʿAlī his children will wear it.'

Special emphasis in Sufism is given to the forty Sacred Traditions, in which the Divine speaks in the first person singular through the Prophet, although they are not part of the Quran. The numerous commentaries made upon the Quran by the individual Sufis, and the Traditions concerning the Prophet, are also essential Sufi sources of doctrine. The books of the sayings of the Shi'ite Imams are important, especially those of 'Alī, the first Imam of Shi'ism, which brings Shi'ite Islam very close to Sufism. Another important source is the great wealth of Sufi poetry, above all the *Mathnawī* of Jalāl al-Dīn Rūmī (p. 53), which has been described as virtually a Persian commentary upon the Quran.

Sufism also assimilated concepts through texts which preceded it in time. The criterion for assimilation was that the foreign element preserved and supported the central doctrine of the Unity of Being. The *Enneads* of Plotinus, for instance, was the most complete metaphysical text to reach Islam from the Greeks; and Plotinus was known to Muslims as the 'Shaykh' or spiritual master. Teachings of the Pythagoreans, especially Niomachus, were also assimilated. The writings of Empedocles on cosmology and the sciences of nature received much attention.

The Hermetic writings of the first to fourth centuries AD, preserving the inner dimension of the traditions of Egypt and Greece, were translated into Arabic; one treatise which appears over and over again is the *Poimandres* attributed to Hermes Trismegistus, the founder of Hermeticism. Hermes is traditionally related to Enoch, and appears in the Quran as the Prophet Idris.

Zoroastrianism, the religion of ancient Iran, also influenced Sufism. The twin concepts 'There is law in Nature. There is conflict in Nature' helped to develop the great Sufi cosmological themes. The Master of Illumination, Shihāb al-Dīn Yaḥyā Suhrawardī, extended certain Zoroastrian ideas in his angelology of lights.

Sufism spiritualized myths and legends from pre-Islamic times, from Persian, Arabic and other sources, by expounding their inner significance. Stories about the Buddha were assimilated: Avicenna based his story 'Salman and Absal' on them.

Returning to Quranic sources, the major Old Testament prophets and the sayings of David and Solomon were very important to Islam in general and to Sufism. The Virgin Mary (p. 82), and the miracle of the virgin birth of Christ, the Word of God, as contained in the Quran, are important Sufi symbols of aspects of the Truth: for the birth of the Word to the Virgin Mary is as the birth of the Word to the unlettered Prophet. The miracle of Islam is the Quran, as the miracle of Christianity is the Christ.

THE CONTAINER AND THE CONTAINED

Every spiritual way emphasizes a particular aspect of the Truth. Christianity, for example, is essentially a way of love; the Christian is tied to Christ through love. To the Sioux, on the other hand, the most important element is self-renunciation. Islam emphasizes knowledge. Sufism begins with the way of knowledge, but carries it to its highest form, knowledge which illuminates.

The way to illumination is often described as consisting of three attainments: the Knowledge of Certainty, the Eye of Certainty, the Truth of Certainty. The distinction may be understood by taking fire as the symbol of Truth. To attain the Knowledge of Certainty is to know fire after having heard it described. To attain the Eye of Certainty is to know fire from seeing the light of its flames. The highest attainment, the Truth of Certainty, belongs to those who know fire from having been consumed in it.

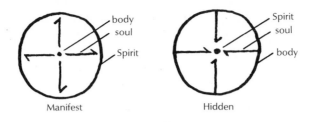

Manifest   Hidden

Knowledge of Certainty is gained from knowing the doctrine of the spiritual path. This forms the body or *container* of Sufism. The Eye of Certainty consists in the spiritual methods and practices *contained* within the body of Sufism, which lead to the Truth of Certainty, knowledge which illuminates. The relationship of the three attainments may be visualized as that of the circumference, radius and centre of a circle. One who attains the Knowledge of Certainty is in the position shown in the first diagram: the aspect of the Manifest, in which one relates to the world outside through the universe, seen in cosmology as the Universal Soul, to its outer limits where it is encompassed by the Universal Spirit. One who attains the Truth of Certainty is in the aspect of the Hidden, in which one relates inwardly from the body or form through the soul to the inmost centre. The movement is through the contained (which exists between circumference and centre) to the Spirit or Secret (*sirr*), the centre of consciousness which is the point of contact between an individual and the Divine Principle.

The gaining of doctrine is thus a centrifugal learning process, outward from the individual human form; the gaining of method is a centripetal learning process which must be actually experienced in order that the knowledge gained through doctrine may illuminate. Through spiritual practices one gains concentrative contemplation and thereby discovers the inner microcosmic Secret.

By incorporating these two diagrams into one we can describe Sufism. The outermost circumference is as the Law of Islam, the *Sharīʿat*. All Sufi doctrine originates implicitly and/or explicitly from here. The need for the Divine Law is often compared to Noah's Ark, which one must, like Noah, build out of planks and dowels. The planks are 'knowledges' and the dowels are actions. Without the Ark, one is drowned in the flood of materiality, as was Noah's son who refused the Law brought by his father.

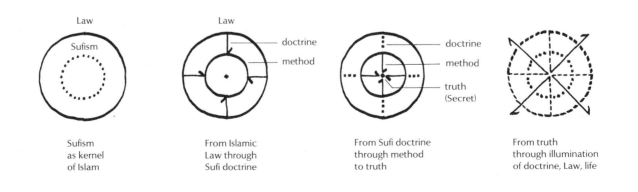

Sufism as kernel of Islam   From Islamic Law through Sufi doctrine   From Sufi doctrine through method to truth   From truth through illumination of doctrine, Law, life

Standing on the circumference of Sufism one relates in an outward direction through the manifest world. The motion inwards is through the spiritual methods which lead to the centre, Secret or Spirit which resides in a state of potentiality in all things. Through an awakening to consciousness of the inner meaning of religious practices and rites, one becomes aware of that which is hidden, for the Spirit exists whether or not we are conscious of it; if we remain unaware, it remains passive and unactivated, only an allusion to the potentiality we contain.

The doctrine and method of Sufism are based on two concepts. Originating from the Quran, these are the two testimonies by which one declares oneself to be a Muslim:

لَا آلِهَ اِلَّا اللّٰهُ مُحَمَّدٌ رَسُولُ اللّٰهِ

Lā ilāha illaʾ Llah
There is no god but God

Muḥammad rasulaʾ Llah
Muḥammad is the Prophet of God

'There is no god but God' and 'Muḥammad is the Prophet of God'. The first expresses the concept of the Unity of Being which annihilates all multiplicity, all separate entities. It is to see, in a sense, the common denominator in all the multiplicities of forms, to see the 'unity in multiplicity' of flower, tree and bird; to see that all circles have a centre regardless of size. The realization of this concept annihilates multiplicity so that unity subsists.

The second testimony expresses the concept of the Universal Prototype (most often translated as the Universal Man). Through this concept one comes to see 'multiplicity in unity'; to recognize the centre of the circle as a unity containing all the multiplicities and accidents possible in the material world; to know that multiplicity subsists only because the unity within subsists.

The Unity of Being

Beginning with the statement of belief, 'There is no god but God' and the Quranic verse, 'Say: God is One' (112:1), the doctrine of the Unity of Being is the basis of Sufi metaphysics. Maḥmūd Shabistarī, in his beautiful *Garden of Mystery*, says simply: 'See One. Say One. Know One.'

Sufis recognize both the immanence and the transcendence of God at one and the same time, and express this in their doctrine. At the same time as God is immanent, God is absolutely transcendent. At the same time as God is 'nearer . . . than the jugular vein' (50:16), God is above every form, thought or thing in the universe, as described in the Throne Verse (2:256). There is a coincidence of opposites here which can be known only through the Intellect or Spirit which shows itself to the mystic through spiritual intuition.

The mystic begins with reason, the light of which is a mere candle when placed next to the Intellect, seen as the light of the sun. We need the candle when beginning the journey in the darkness of the wilderness, but once the illumination of the sun rises, we put the candle aside.

Sufism is not a philosophy, in that it is based on the nature of Reality which is transcendent. All purely philosophical systems are necessarily closed, since no mental form can encompass the Infinite: mental form itself is part of the Infinite. It is only the

We indeed created man; and We know what his soul whispers within him, and We are nearer to him than the jugular vein.

Quran 50:16,
trans. A. J. Arberry

God
*there is no god but He, the
Living, the Everlasting.
Slumber seizes Him not, neither sleep;
to Him belongs
all that is in the heavens and the earth.
Who is there that shall intercede with Him
save by His Leave?
He knows what lies before them and what is after them,
and they comprehend not anything of His knowledge
save such as He wills.
His Throne comprises the heavens and earth;
the preserving of them oppresses Him not;
He is the All-high, the All-glorious.*

Quran 2:256,
trans. A. J. Arberry

spiritual Heart, the instrument of intuition, which is above forms and capable of holding the Throne of God.

At one and the same time, the Sufi realizes an outer state of knowledge beyond the Divine Law and seeks union with the inner Truth through meditation and invocation of the Divine Name (p. 39). The one who attains is the one who knows *through* God, after travelling *to* God, *in* God. The goal of the Quest is for self to step aside and let the Absolute know Itself through Itself. As Farīd al-Dīn ʿAṭṭār says (pp. 36–37): 'The pilgrim, the pilgrimage and the Way are but a journey from self to Self.'

The goal of Sufism is to gather all multiplicity into unity, with the totality of one's being, in direct contemplation of spiritual realities; to come to know the qualitative unity which transcends the existence it unifies, at the same time as one integrates all aspects of self into a centre.

The journey begins with withdrawal from the material world in which one is drowned. To go from multiplicity-in-unity to unity-in-multiplicity, one must first die to self: not a biological death but a spiritual one, where the soul dies, and by dying is transformed, and then returns to this material world.

At this moment the multiplicity of the soul (the sensory and psychic forces) disappears, and the vision of Unity fills the emptied soul. This is when one sees God in Oneness. Then, when one returns to consciousness of multiplicity, the Spirit returns to all things.

The ultimate meaning of the Unity of Being is 'to see things as they really are': to realize that all is reflected in the mirror of one's own being. It is the dissolution of the profane consciousness of man who sees all things as independent of God: to realize that one was never separate from God; that God in His Oneness is both immanent and transcendent.

Come you lost atoms, to your Centre draw
And be the Eternal Mirror that you saw:
Rays that have wander'd into Darkness wide
Return and back into your Sun subside.

Farīd al-Dīn ʿAṭṭār,
'Mantiq al-Tayr'.

I died from mineral, and plant became;
Died from the plant and took a sentient frame;
Died from the beast, and donned a human dress;
When by my dying did I e'er grow less:
Another time from manhood I must die
To soar with angel-pinions through the sky.
'Midst Angels also I must lose my place
Since 'Everything shall perish save His Face.'
Let me be Naught! The harp-strings tell me plain
That unto Him do we return again!

Jalāl al-Dīn Rūmī, 'Mathnawī',
trans. E. G. Browne.

Know that the world is a mirror from head to foot,
In every atom are a hundred blazing suns.
If you cleave the heart of one drop of water,
A hundred pure oceans emerge from it.
If you examine closely each grain of sand,
A thousand Adams may be seen in it.
In its members a gnat is like an elephant,
In its qualities a drop of rain is like the Nile.
The heart of a piece of corn equals a hundred harvests,
A world dwells in the heart of a millet seed.
In the wing of a gnat is the ocean of life.
In the pupil of the eye a heaven.
What though the corn grain of the heart be small
It is a station of the Lord of both worlds to dwell therein.

Maḥmūd Shabistarī,
'Gulshan-i-rāz'
(The Garden of Mystery).

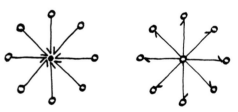

Multiplicity in unity   Unity in multiplicity

The Universal Prototype

In order to come to know the Unity of Being, to realize the coincidence of its opposite aspects, transcendence and immanence, one needs a spiritual method. The method of Sufism is derived from the second testimony of Islam, 'Muḥammad is the Prophet of God'. The Prophet serves as the spiritual model by which one seeks to achieve the coincidence of opposites within self (p. 35). He serves as the place of gathering of all those universal and particular forms and meanings which are displayed throughout the universe (p. 87).

As the founder of Islam, his role follows that of other Prophets who preceded him in time (p. 97). The founder of every religious tradition is said to be an aspect of the Divine Word, the Universal Logos. Although the Prophet was the last prophet in the present cycle of existence, and is thereby known as the Seal of Prophecy, in essence he was the first. This refers us to a Tradition in which he says: 'I was the Logos when Adam was

Immanence

Transcendence

between water and clay.' In essence, the Divine Idea of the last prophet, Muḥammad (ﷺ), preceded the first to come into actual existence, Adam, as a thought is completed before it is actualized.

The Prophet is an individual who, in form, manifests all the possibilities of humanity. By marrying and having children, he expresses his human nature. Through his receiving the revelation while in an unlettered or virgin state, he is the receptacle of Divine nature. The Prophet, referring to this aspect of himself, has said, 'I am Aḥmad without the *m* [*Aḥad* means Unity]; I am an *'arab* without the *'a* [*rabb* means Lord]; who hath seen me hath seen the Truth.' The Prophet is the Universal Prototype who unites the inward, eternal aspect of reality with the outward, phenomenal aspect. The Universal Prototype comprehends all individualities and unites all opposites in the infinite and universal nature of Self. All Divine Qualities are united and displayed. Hence the Prototype becomes the means through which the artisan or architect comes to display the splendour of creation.

Ibn 'Arabī says: 'The Universal Prototype stands in the same relation to God as the pupil which is the instrument of vision to the eye. Through the Universal Prototype, God becomes conscious of Self in all the Divine aspects. The Universal Prototype is the eye of the world, whereby the Absolute sees Its own works.'

The Universal Prototype or Logos symbolizes four aspects of Divine manifestation. The Logos is the 'uncreated', pre-existent aspect within things: in the move towards creation it is the firstborn of God, the first to contain 'thingness'. The Logos is also Light: when chaos, the abysmal darkness, ended and moved towards order, Light came into being, of which wisdom is only a reflection. The Logos is also the active agent in the work of creation, the creative directing principle of the universe. Finally, the Logos is the prototypical human form. It is God's own image, the centre of the universe and the Spirit of the Absolute. It is the Word made manifest.

The possibility of becoming the Universal Prototype exists potentially for all Muslims. The difference between one who is awakened and one who remains asleep, and the difference in the levels attained by the awakened, depend upon what Sufis call preparedness. This preparedness is one's primordial nature. A comparison with light and with water is often made to further describe this term. All are potentially as unified white light which, when passed through a prism, assumes a variety of colours which existed in potential in the very nature of the light itself. The potential within light or within self, the preparedness of the human form, determines the ability to actualize spiritual intuition. In the same sense: water appears as water, but its taste varies according to the place from which it has been gathered, as primordial nature varies from form to form although outwardly not apparent.

Each Sufi seeks to become the Universal Prototype. The method of attainment is invocation (p. 39), a process which must continue until one can be described by the Sacred Tradition in which God says, 'My servant never ceases drawing nigh unto Me, and when my servant does so, I become the Hearing by which he hears, the Seeing by which he sees, the Hand by which he seizes and the Foot by which he walks.' The Sufi 'witnesses' when in full consciousness of the Divine Presence (pp. 102–3). To do so is to 'worship God as if you saw Him, and if you do not see Him [know intuitively], He sees you'. It is to know that God is always in the direction towards which one prays and invokes.

CREATION: THE ARC OF DESCENT

arc
of descent

Sufis often refer to the saying 'God spreads the scrolls upon the heavens until man learns to read them. Once he can read them, he can roll up the scrolls and put them away.' The cosmos, known to mystics as a veil, as allusion, and as separation, is referred to in the Quranic verse, 'We shall show them our symbols in the horizons and in themselves, until it be made known to them that it is the Truth' (41:53).

The cosmos has two aspects. Known through the Tradition 'God created seventy thousand veils of Light and Darkness', the first is expressed in the statement that the universe is not God. The universe is relative, transient, changing; therefore it is otherness, separateness, a veil which separates us from God. In its other aspect, the universe is none other than God, because it is the universe which reveals the Divinity. Therefore, the cosmos both hides and reveals, veils and makes manifest. To the Sufi, the world is transparent, because the Sufi sees the transcendent significance of physical things, and this is expressed and reflected in art (p. 33).

In a sense, the cosmos falls between the concept of the Unity of Being, expressed as multiplicity in unity, and that of the Universal Prototype, expressed as unity in multiplicity. The cosmos is both container, expression of the Unity of Being, and contained, expression of the Universal Prototype.

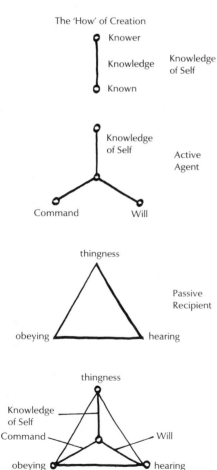

The 'Why' of Creation

There is a Sacred Tradition in which the Divine says: 'I was a Hidden Treasure. I desired to be known, so I created the universe.' The drama of creation takes place from Not-Being to Being, from 'desire' to 'being known'. The Divine conceives of the possibilities contained within Itself and then brings them forth. It is, in a sense, the Mystery as it steps out of the primordial darkness into Light.

Why should an Absolute and Infinite Reality express Itself? Hindus say that the question is essentially unanswerable, and therefore they refer to 'Divine play'. Some other religions, including the exoteric traditions of Islam, relate it to the imponderable element of the Divine Will. Sufism answers: 'For Knowledge of Self.' Each form re-expressed, recalled, remembered, is so that It may come to know Self.

Since the Divine is Infinite, Knowledge of Self is a part of Its Infiniteness. Being Infinite and Absolute, containing the totality of possibilities, It must include the possibility of negating Self and bringing the relative into being. Therefore the world exists because God is Infinite.

The 'How' of Creation

The 'how' of creation is conceived as a triplicity. The number One is perfect and beyond description. It is the principle and origin of all numbers. The first odd number then is not one, but three. Three is conceived of as the level of singleness, which is the Absolute 'with knowledge': being 'with knowledge' necessarily implies three – knower, knowledge and known (a subject, a motion and an object).

Creation begins with the One at the point when It has singleness. This singleness has another three aspects which participate in the process of creation. First, there arises Knowledge of Self within the One as It moves towards manifestation. At this moment, the Archetypes (a'yān thābitah) or Divine Names and Qualities appear in Divine Consciousness. This marks the birth of multiplicity. Essence, the Hidden Treasure, moves to the level of the Divinity. Subsequent to this, there arises the Will, based on knowledge, to bring the Archetypes from non-existence (phenomenally) to phenomenal existence. On the basis of the Divine Will, the Command 'Be!' is issued and the universe is created.

The above triplicity of Self-Knowledge (itself a triplicity of knower, knowledge and known), Will and Command, concerns the Agent. This alone does not produce any effect. In order for the Agent to be effective, there must be a recognition of the corresponding mode of triplicity on the part of the receiver, 'that which is to become known'. Creation can be actualized only when the two triplicities, active and passive, coincide. Ibn 'Arabī expresses this in the following way:

'Looking at an artisan [knower] who is engaged in moulding things out of clay [that which is to be known], one might make a superficial observation that the clay in the hands of an artisan is sheer passivity, sheer non-action. One overlooks the important fact that, in reality, the clay for its own part positively determines the activity of the artisan. Surely, the artisan can make a variety of things out of clay, but, whatever one may do, one cannot go beyond the narrow limits set by the very nature of the clay. Otherwise expressed, the nature of the clay itself determines the possible forms in which it may be actualized.' (T. Izutsu.)

At the moment when the Word 'Be!' is Commanded of a thing, there arises in it a singleness which contains a triplicity. It is this triplicity contained within the receiving form which allows a thing to be qualified by existence. The first element in the triplicity, described as 'the archetypal essence of a thing which is in a state of non-existence waiting to be known', corresponds to Self-Knowledge on the part of the Agent. The hearing on the part of the recipient corresponds to the Will of the Agent. The obedience to what is Commanded corresponds to the Command which issues the Word 'Be!' 'Whenever We decide something,' God says in the Quran, 'We only say to it "Be!", and it comes into existence.' (16:40.) The thing, in response, comes into being through its own act, not the act of God.

The World of Archetypes. Every religion needs a language to express the motion from the One to the many. In Sufism, the language of expression is that of the Archetypes or Divine Names and Qualities.

The Godhead in Its unmanifest quality is above every quality we could ascribe to It. This is the Divine Essence about which one can say nothing, for any description would only serve to limit or bind It. Divine Essence manifests Itself, however, in the direction of Creation through stages, the first of which is the Archetypes, the possibilities contained within the Absolute.

Divine emanation is a twofold process: intelligible and sensible. The first emanation brings the Archetypes into intelligible existence. Known as the Divine Names and Qualities, these Archetypes are the possibilities contained within the Absolute. They occupy a middle position between the Absolute and the sensible world. They are passive in relation to the Absolute, at the same time as they are active in relation to the worlds below them. They are actualized in the sensible, phenomenal world according to the preparedness of the particular sensible form which they take on: Ibn 'Arabī's 'nature of the clay itself'.

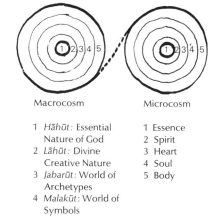

Macrocosm   Microcosm

1 *Hāhūt:* Essential   1 Essence
   Nature of God   2 Spirit
2 *Lāhūt:* Divine   3 Heart
   Creative Nature   4 Soul
3 *Jabarūt:* World of   5 Body
   Archetypes
4 *Malakūt:* World of
   Symbols
5 *Nāsūt:* human nature

In Sufism, it is through the Archetypes as Names of God (p. 39) that one invokes, calls upon, the Absolute, whether one is transforming one's own soul or the soul of a particular object. As the Names are the hierarchies of being between us and the Absolute, their existence is essential both to veil the light of the Absolute and to serve as a bridge between us and the Divine Essence (pp. 33, 43).

Revealed through the Quran, itself meaning 'Recite!' – 'To God belong the Names Most Beautiful, so call Him by them' (7:179) – the ninety-nine Names are divided into various forms. Often they are classified as Names of Essence, of Actions and of Qualities. Names of Essence, such as *Ahad*, the One, *Ḥaqq*, the Truth or Absolute, *Nūr*, Light and *Allāh*, God (p. 34), concern the Divinity and would exist whether or not there had been a creation. They are aspects completely independent of us. Names of Actions, such as *Khalq*, Creator, depend upon creation. Names of Qualities include *Karīm*, Generous, *Ḥayy*, Living, and *Shakūr*, Thankful. The Names are also classified as Names of Majesty (*Jalāl*) and Names of Beauty (*Jamāl*) (pp. 66, 67). The mystic invokes God through the Names of Beauty, because they symbolize ascent, whereas the Names of Majesty refer to the descent of creation.

This stage of emanation is conceived of as the One (*Aḥadiyyah*) moving towards Oneness (*Wāḥīdiyyah*); the Archetypes are noumena, forms which are outwardly and actually intelligible, but inwardly and potentially sensible.

The second stage of emanation occurs when the shadows of the Archetypes reach the world of symbols (*ʿālam-i-mithāl*) and the shadows of the world of symbols reach the phenomenal world. The phenomenal world is a manifestation of these higher worlds and reflects the splendour of multiplicity. The phenomenon is a form which is outwardly and actually sensible: it can be grasped by the five outer senses of sight, hearing, smell, taste and touch. Outward forms act as sensible containers for the Archetypes, which are in turn intelligible containers for aspects of the Absolute.

The transitional world of symbols is that by virtue of which sensible forms (the measurable) correspond exactly to intellections (the unmeasurable). Form is the philosopher's stone without which there can be no transformation. That is, 'I' can mentally comprehend an idea without a form, but 'I' can actualize my own transformation only by the practice of rites in the presence of symbolic forms.

The literal making of sensible forms is important because without the expression of the potentiality, the preparedness (*istiʿdād*), within 'that which is to be known', nature would lie passive and dormant. By acting on this preparedness the artisan brings forth the Spirit within, whether it be in the creation of a carpet, a brass tray or a miniature.

The Shadow of the Absolute. The universe in Sufi terminology is often referred to as the shadow of the Absolute: something which has relative existence by virtue of being a sensible determination of an Archetype.

The relation between a shadow and that which casts it is like the relation of the phenomenon to the cause of its noumenon. In order to have a shadow, one must have three things: first, something which will cast a shadow; second, a place where the shadow may fall; and third, light by which the shadow is made known. In Sufi terminology, it is the Absolute in the relative aspect of Self which casts the shadow. The place is the world of Archetypes, the place of the essences of possible things. If there were no place, the shadow would remain intelligible only, like a seed in a tree. The Light by which the shadow is made known is a manifestation of the Absolute as well. Shining

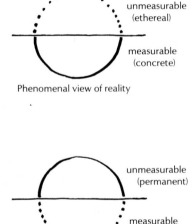

unmeasurable (ethereal)

measurable (concrete)

Phenomenal view of reality

unmeasurable (permanent)

measurable (changing)

Noumenal view of reality

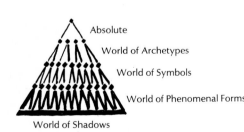

Absolute

World of Archetypes

World of Symbols

World of Phenomenal Forms

World of Shadows

on the world of Archetypes, it casts a shadow on the lower world of symbols which finally reach the phenomenal world. If the upper world did not veil the Light, and cast the shadow which is all that we see, the Light would be blinding.

A shadow is explained as being the extent of the distance between that which has light as its manifested form, like the sun, whose light is of itself, and the light which the moon, in its receptive quality, reflects.

The absence of shadow in Persian miniatures reveals that they spring from the world of Archetypes which reflects the Light from the Divine. Below this world is the world of shadows. It is for this reason that the miniature also ignores perspective, for perspective is a sensible phenomenon far from the world of Archetypes: it creates an artificial imagination by describing a third dimension too clearly, and the sense of personal discovery is removed. Architecture, on the other hand, is devoted to creating shadows, for architecture is part of this phenomenal world, and catches the light and casts shadows, whereas the miniature reflects pure light.

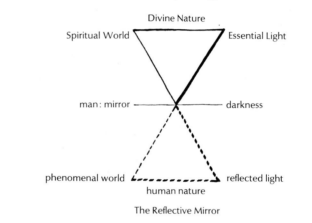

The Reflective Mirror

The Reflective Mirror. A second concept of creation important to Sufi expression is that of the mirror. Before the creation of human beings, the universe had been brought into being, but it was unpolished, unreflective, unconscious of the Divine Presence. The macrocosmic universe came into being so that the manifestation of Self in the form of a Divine Name would have a 'place'. However, each Name has a particular form, so that there arose a multiplicity of particulars. There was no place for all the particular forms to gather into a unity, so mankind served to polish the mirror. This polishing by mankind occurs through unified consciousness of the Divine Presence as It manifests Itself within all forms. All other beings reflect only single Qualities of the Absolute. Together they form a Unity, but without consciousness the Unity is not perfect and complete.

The mystic aspires to become this reflective mirror. Polishing the mirror in order to make it a place for the Divine Self to see Self depends upon two modes: the first, the 'preparedness' of the place, is the ability to receive, conceive and give birth to the second mode, the descent of one of the Divine Names.

The Sufi thus becomes the instrument by which the Divine can have a vision of Self in another form. The mystic, empty of self, then has the capacity to reflect the Divine to the Divine. The mystic has been unveiled so that Light comes to reflect Light, Presence witnesses Presence, and the 'desire' for the Name to be known is made manifest.

form

expansion

contraction

The Breath of the
Compassionate

To the Sufi, creative expression which results from *participation mystique* – that is, a state of being one with nature, although not conscious of the Divine Presence – is an expression of one's vision of self within self. It is an expression which is not reflective, not polished, not aware of the total possibilities inherent in the nature of things. It is only through conscious expression that one has the more perfect vision of self reflected in the qualities of something else. The only way that expression can serve in its full capacity is when it is reflective; it becomes reflective only when conscious of the Divine Presence. The reflective surface now reflects something which is contained, a Spirit which is not only one's own. This is the Spirit which is universal to all things: to the Sufi, it is the 'desire' which exists within things 'to be known'.

The Breath of the Compassionate. The preparedness within a thing, its inner Archetype, is actualized in an intelligible form at the moment when its Name flows into it through a Word. The Divine Spirit or Logos flows into a thing through the process of the Divine Breath, the Breath of the Divine Name *Raḥmān*, Compassionate. The Name of the Compassionate (p. 55), manifested through the Divine Breath, is just one of the many symbolic processes which the traditional craftsman emulates. By blowing or chanting the Divine Names upon the form to be transformed, the creative process of the breath, which contains the Divine Presence through a Name, transforms the object in hand. The creator participates as active agent and the object participates as passive recipient.

There is a Tradition of the Prophet in which he says: 'God created the universe through the Breath of the Compassionate.' The Compassionate (*Raḥmān*) is the highest of the Names, Ideas or Archetypes. 'Where was your Lord before creating the visible Creation?' someone asked the Prophet. His answer: 'In a cloud. There was no space either above or below.' This cloud which the Divine Being exhaled, and in which It originally was, receives all forms at the same time as It gives beings their forms. It is the act of making things to exist. The Absolute, appearing in the Name, Compassion, overflowing with goodness, gives existence without limit and without end.

When the desire to be known, the preparedness, arises within a thing, the Divine as Compassion extends Itself as Archetype to the thing and becomes its receptivity, its ability to receive the theophany. This receptivity is actually what the Archetype, in its state of concrete essence, desires. Therefore, the actual effect of Compassion is to give a thing the possibility of receiving sensible existence. Compassion is given without any discrimination; Mercy, the complement, is given only for an act done. Compassion, in a sense, is the universal form of Divine giving; Mercy is the particular aspect.

Through the Name of Compassion, the Absolute breathes out upon the other Names or Archetypes. This breathing out is a means of bringing things into existence. By means of the Command 'Be!' the Absolute through Compassion sends into the external, phenomenal world that which has been compressed within It.

The Divine Breath pervades the Universe. Just as breath is exhaled and so forms syllables and words, the Breath of the Compassionate, in exhaling Words (intelligible forms), brings the sensible form into being.

This Divine Breath is Nature itself. Just as the Breath contains all the forms of the universe in a potential state and actualizes them by exhaling, so Nature holds all forms of expression in a potential state of preparedness in which they await the appearance of the Breath of the Compassionate, the Spirit, the Logos, in order to be known.

This Breath is essentially the initial act of the metaphysic of love. Love is the cause and secret of all creation and thereby the principle of all motion from desire to being known. The creation of the world, in this sense, was the motion of love towards perfection and completion. The Absolute loves to be perfect in both types of forms: intelligible and sensible.

Ultimately, one who wishes to know the Breath of the Compassionate need only know Self, for Self is the Lord who is manifested in the form. One's innermost being is most directly expressed through speech. Speech on the human plane reflects the Divine Word or Logos; it was the Word that created the universe and it is through the Word that it returns to God. Invocation (*zikr*) is the means of reaching the very substance of things within us.

Everything contains the Presence of the Divine. The ideas or intellections in *our* minds are like those Ideas in the mind of the Absolute. A word contains both a meaning and the thing itself, which has a form. The meaning is permanent, the Divine Idea; the form the thing takes is but a shadow, transient. The Ideas are made temporal through the Breath of the Compassionate. In Sufism, Christ symbolizes the particular Divine Quality of the Breath of the Compassionate, for it is through the Breath that all things receive life. 'When the Word of God comes into the heart of anyone and the Divine Inspiration enters his heart and his soul, its nature is such that there is produced in him a spiritual child having the breath of Jesus that revives the dead.' (R. Nicholson, *Mathnawī*.)

The 'What' of Creation

The universe, in the Sufi view, is being re-created at every moment. At every moment what appears to be a time-connected universe returns to God. There is continuous, instantaneous expansion and contraction.

The manifestation of actualized individual things occurs continually, as in successive waves. At every moment creation is annihilated and re-created. With each heartbeat we die and are reborn. The world is in intense motion, ascending towards the vertical axis within all things to meet the descent of the Absolute in manifested forms. The flow occurs in such an orderly, successive manner, according to definite patterns, that we are unaware of it, and the world appears to us to stay the same. This ever-new creation is a process which only the human form endowed with consciousness of Self can come to know. Arabesque patterns, in rugs or in tiles, witness this concept of constant flux. As Ibn ʿArabī expressed it:

'The wonder of wonders is that the human form and all other created things are in a perpetual process of ascending. And yet one is not ordinarily aware of this because of the extreme thinness and fineness of the veil (when one looks at something through a very transparent veil, one does not become aware of the veil between oneself and the object) or because of the extreme similarity between the successive forms. How splendid is God's description of the universe, and of its perpetual renewal with each Divine Breath which constitutes an ever new creation in one single entity! But this is perceived by only a few, as the Quran says: '"Nay, they are in utter confusion regarding the new creation"' (50:15). These people who do not perceive are in confusion because they do not know the constant renewal of things with each Divine Breath.' (T. Izutsu.)

The Sufi, whether or not expressing forms outside of self, is aware of the constantly changing forms of the Divine. We come to know the changing forms by realizing that we are ourselves constantly changing from one form to another. Knowledge of this constant transformation of self into a myriad modes and states leads to knowledge of the Divine as It goes on transforming Itself moment after moment in all the possible forms of the world. This is expressed in the arabesque and in all rhythmic art forms, where, each time one looks, one sees another facet.

THE HUMAN SOUL

It is the soul, the feminine principle between body and Spirit, which undertakes the Quest and is transformed (see pp. 84–92) from its physical and sensible function to its psychic function and thence to its spiritual function. As the soul approaches the second transformation, from sensible to spiritual, it becomes what the Sufi calls the spiritual Heart, the instrument of intuition. It is the Heart which finally unites with the Spirit. It is annihilated and experiences a spiritual death. It is then reborn with the Spirit and attains subsistence: it knows that it exists through the Absolute and was never really separated from It.

The soul has its origin in the spiritual world. When it is attached to the body, it descends from the world of Light to this world of darkness, dark because of its distance from the Source. If the body with its desires proves the stronger, the soul becomes heavier, more materially oriented, dense and opaque. The veils multiply. If, however, this soul becomes aware of its captivity and conscious of its imprisonment within the six directions of the body and the four primary elements of earth, air, water and fire, then and only then can the journey of the feminine principle begin.

Having fallen into the world against its will, it finds itself a stranger, an exile from the world of Light. The soul must raise itself to the level where it feels its chains and bonds to be intolerable, and then, with the aid of its spiritual faculties, which only now realize the bondage, free itself and return whence it came. Thus, the moment of consciousness is awareness of the exile, the moment when the soul realizes the illusion of this life and yearns to return to its Origin where it was one with the light of Unity. Only then does the mystic's soul discover where it is, where it came from and where it is to go.

The human form contains the possibility of uniting the opposites within by means of consciousness. The soul, the feminine principle of the reflective moon within, is united with the Spirit or Intellect, the masculine principle of the sun within (pp. 60–61). Then the 'desire', which sought knowledge, becomes known. Then one has realized the Tradition of the Prophet, 'one who knows self, knows Lord'. The Way of Sufism is to become aware of the possibilities which exist within the human form, to conceive them, and then through spiritual practices to actualize them. Ibn ʿArabī says: 'Remove from your thought the exterior of words; seek the interior until you understand.' (H. Corbin, *Creative Imagination*. . . .)

The soul consists of a threefold hierarchical structure: sensory, psychic and spiritual. The soul in its sensory and psychic form is the soul existent within the human form. We can, through structural analogy, relate the human form or microcosm to a circle, where the circumference is the physical, the radii are the sensory-psychic area, and the centre is the spiritual. The space between the centre and the circumference is the place to which the soul descends at conception.

It descended upon thee from out of the regions above,
That exalted, ineffable, glorious, heavenly Dove.
'Twas concealed from the eyes of all those who its
    nature would ken
Yet it wears not a veil, and is ever apparent to men.
Unwilling it sought thee and joined thee, and yet,
    though it grieve,
It is like to be still more unwilling thy body to leave.
It resisted and struggled, and would not be tamed in
    haste,
Yet it joined thee, and slowly grew used to this desolate
    waste,
Till, forgotten at length, as I ween, were haunts and its
    troth
In the heavenly gardens and groves, which to leave it
    was loath.
Until, when it entered the D of its downward Descent,
And to earth, to the C of its centre, unwillingly went,
The eye of (I) infirmity smote it, and lo, it was hurled
Midst the sign-posts and ruined abodes of this desolate
    world.
It weeps, when it thinks of its home and the peace it
    possessed,
With tears welling forth from its eyes without pausing
    or rest,
And with plaintive mourning it broodeth like one bereft
O'er such trace of its home as the fourfold winds have
    left.
Thick nets detain it, and strong is the cage whereby
It is held from seeking the lofty and spacious sky.
Until, when the hour of its homeward flight draws near,
And 'tis time for it to return to its ampler sphere,
It carols with joy, for the veil is raised, and it spies
Such things as cannot be witnessed by waking eyes.
On a lofty height doth it warble its songs of praise
(For even the lowliest being doth knowledge raise).
And so it returneth, aware of all hidden things
In the universe, while no stain to its garment clings.

Now why from its perch on high was it cast like this
To the lowest Nadir's gloomy and drear abyss?
Was it God who cast it forth for some purpose wise,
Concealed from the keenest seeker's inquiring eyes?
Then is its descent a disciple wise but stern,
That the things that it hath not heard it thus may learn.
So 'tis she whom Fate doth plunder, while her star
Setteth at length in a place from its rising far,
Like a gleam of lightning which over the meadows
    shone,
And, as though it ne'er had been, in a moment is gone.

Ibn Sīnā (Avicenna),
'Ode to the Human Soul',
trans. E. G. Browne.

Having come from the non-physical world, it must first of all become less subtle and more concrete. In this process, it becomes the vegetative soul (nafs-i-nabātiyyah), allowing the form within the womb to have the same function of feeding and growth that plants have: the ability to transform foreign substances into its own form.

As the form grows in the womb, it develops the animal soul (nafs-i-ḥayawāniyyah), in which it acquires the ability of motion. At birth, the animal soul is completed, as the form exhibits various desires. However, not until adolescence does the soul pass from potential consciousness to being able to actualize consciousness with the appearance of the rational soul (nafs-i-nāṭiqah). The Quest may begin now. The ability to transform self has come into existence.

The first stage of the journey is to retrace one's steps, to return to one's primordial nature (fiṭrat), to become a form without desires. That is, one actively denies self-desires, and exists with the faculties of feeding, growth, motion and the ability to transform foreign substances into one's own form. It is a return to complete potentiality before any masks were assumed. To be awakened is to cross the bridge to one's primordial nature and then enter through the gateway (pp. 42–43).

The Sensory Structure

Once inside the gateway the mystic encounters the five senses, the physical instruments of the sensory structure. Whereas the first stage consists of denial and asceticism, the second is saturation. An eleventh-century commentator upon one of Avicenna's mystical recitals says: 'Know that access to that by which our soul becomes knowing begins by way of the senses; so long as we do not perceive sensible things – the visible, the audible, the sapid, the odorous, and the tangible – knowledge is out of our reach.' (H. Corbin, Avicenna. . . .)

This is perhaps the most treacherous part of the journey, for one is often waylaid by the sensory pleasures and detained from journeying further. Desires of the carnal soul reappear as the dragon (p. 45), and one must fight one's way forward. Suhrawardī admonishes the mystic to move forward quickly, as these pleasures are only dim lights in comparison with the remainder of the journey.

The Psychic Structure

The psychic aspect of the feminine principle consists of the five internal senses: common sense, imagination, intelligence, memory, and Active Imagination or Intellect. The functions of these internal senses are described according to form (hayūlā) and meaning (ma'nā). That is, common sense is the ability to perceive the forms of things, whereas imagination is the ability to perceive meanings. When one has perceived both form and meaning, both these psychic structures are operative. One who sees only form without meaning, or meaning without form, needs to develop the complement. Intelligence is the ability to preserve forms, and memory is the ability to preserve meanings. These two functions play a very important role in contemplation. The fifth psychic structure is known by many names: it is the intuitive ability to govern both sensible phenomena and intelligible noumena so that a balance is always preserved.

Sufis call it the spiritual Heart. This function, containing both the feminine principle (as manifested in the sensible) and the masculine principle (as manifested in the intelligible), must activate and join the two. It is to this faculty that the Angel Gabriel (p. 76) relates, by bringing either revelation, which was given to the Prophets, or inspiration, which is still given to the Saints.

This psychic structure of the soul has been expressed by Ghazālī in an esoteric commentary upon the Verse of Light (Quran 24:35). The niche, as a place of gathering of both sound and light in the outer world, is also a place of gathering inwardly for all sensory perceptions. A focus point, an aperture in the wall, it symbolizes the first inner aspect of the soul, common sense. The glass symbolizes the second, imagination, which like glass is part of the materiality of this world and has a definite dimension: like glass in its making, imagination is at first opaque to the light of the Intellect which transcends direction, quality and distance. Once the imagination is clarified and refined, it gains a similarity to the Active Intellect, or spiritual Heart, and becomes transparent to the light. Just as a glass is needed to protect the candlelight from being dissipated by the wind, so the imagination is needed to control intellectual knowledge and hold the images together.

The third symbol, that of the light-giving lamp, is related to the intelligence (that is, the thinking function or the function of will), for it is this faculty which recognizes the Archetypes or Divine Names and Qualities.

The function of meditation (formed by memory) and reflection is symbolized by the fourth symbol, the tree. Meditation begins with a thought and branches out into others: its conclusions become seeds producing the further growth of thought. The tree is not a fruit tree but the olive tree, the oil of which feeds the lamps; and as opposed to other soils, the oil of the olive increases radiance. This is not any tree, any meditation, but rather meditation upon that 'which is neither of the East nor the West'.

The fifth symbol, the oil, relates to the faculty that is sacred within the human form, the spiritual Heart, or Active Imagination, or Active Intellect: the Spirit of God within us. Existing in potential in all human beings, it is actualized and made luminous in but a very few. For most people, the acquisition of knowledge must come from without. The Active Intellect, on the other hand, is self-luminous with no external source: the oil which 'would shine, even if no fire touched it'.

Thus the psyche (the inner senses) is just one part of a larger totality of the feminine principle or soul, incorporating the outer senses, which moves on the mystic Quest towards spiritual becoming and union with the Spirit. It is in this phase of the journey that one meets with the *jinn* (p. 44), the psychic forces within. They constantly intrude with temptations and inclinations which one must actively put aside, or, once again, one will be hindered from continuing the journey.

The Spiritual Becoming

The soul, the feminine principle, the sensible and psychic structure within the human form, is of Divine origin; for God breathed His Spirit into it. Once this feminine principle has been awakened to the realization that it came from some 'place' other than the

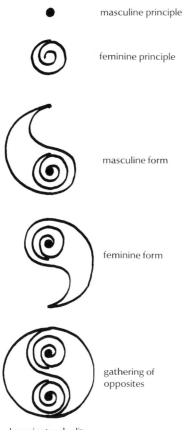

masculine principle

feminine principle

masculine form

feminine form

gathering of opposites

Inner/outer duality

physical world, that the physical world is, in a sense, only an illusion, it is overcome with an ardent desire to be known and in doing so goes through three spiritual stages.

The first stage is the awakening to consciousness of the existence of the passionate, egoistic soul, the soul which commands (*nafs-i-ammārah*). At the second stage, the feminine principle's becoming is called the accusing, reproaching soul (*nafs-i-lawwāmah*), the soul aware of its own imperfections and blaming self. Here the struggle between good and evil is enacted. Finally, the feminine principle reaches the spiritual stage of peace (*nafs-i-muṭa'innah*), when it is reintegrated with the Spirit, the masculine principle, and at rest in certainty. The Quran calls out: 'O soul at peace, return unto thy Lord, well-pleased, well-pleasing. Enter thou among My servants! Enter thou My Paradise!' (39:29.)

The Gathering of Opposites

The human form is the place of gathering (see p. 102). It gathers two separate dualities: an inner and an outer. The inner duality exists *within* the form, and is essentially the vision one has of oneself. The outer duality exists *between* forms; it is the vision one has of oneself as reflected in another form.

In the inner duality, men and women are the same. The meaning of the form does not differ: the masculine and feminine principles of Spirit and soul exist in both, irrespective of the outer form. The differences are between individuals, depending upon capacity and preparedness.

The outer duality consists of the physical forms of man and woman. Concerning the role of the physical forms in spiritual reintegration, Rūmī says: 'The physical form is of great importance; nothing can be done without the consociation of the form and the essence. However often you may sow a seed, stripped of the pod, it will not grow. Sow it with the pod, it will become a great tree. From this point of view, the body is fundamental and necessary for the realization of the Divine intention.' (R. Nicholson, *The Mathnawī*.)

Thus it is only through the form that the gathering of opposites may be accomplished. The form of woman holds the highest essence, and therefore Ibn 'Arabī says: 'Woman is the highest form of earthly beauty, but earthly beauty is nothing unless it is a manifestation and reflection of the Divine Qualities.' It is by means of the symbolic understanding of this feminine form that spiritual transformation is achieved. Ibn 'Arabī continues: 'Know that the Absolute cannot be contemplated independently of a concrete being, and It is more perfectly seen in a human form than in any other, and more perfectly in woman than in man.' (R. Nicholson, *The Mathnawī*.)

The creation of concrete forms, in which one can come to contemplate the Divine, is the very reason for the existence of art. The material in the form created by the artist, and the creative process itself, are aspects of the feminine principle. The maker must play two roles: as a passive recipient to the idea which is conceived and an active agent towards that which is to be born.

As to woman being both active and receptive, Ibn ʿArabī explains further the point that the Absolute is contemplated more perfectly through a woman (p. 69). In the first place, man exists between two feminine principles. The Quran states: 'And He created from Adam his mate and out of the two He spread innumerable men and women' (4:1). Commentators, referring to this verse, say: 'The wife of Adam was feminine, but the first soul from which Adam was born was also feminine.' (T. Izutsu.) That is, Adam (p. 84) exists between two feminine principles: the soul he was born from, and the soul which was born from him.

Secondly, one contemplates the Absolute either in Its aspect of Agent (expressed in poetry as the Lover) or in that of Recipient (expressed in poetry as the Beloved), or both at the same time (p. 92). Thus, when a man contemplates the Absolute in his own form, he sees that the feminine soul was born of the masculine Spirit; this is to contemplate the Absolute as active. Otherwise he may contemplate the Absolute in its passive aspect, because his own form, as a creature, is absolutely passive in relation to the Absolute. But when a man contemplates the Absolute through a woman's outer form, or in a state of meditation upon her inner form, he contemplates both these aspects simultaneously. Ibn ʿArabī describes the process:

'The Absolute manifested in the form of woman is active agent because of exercising complete control over man's feminine principle, his soul. This causes man to become submissive and devoted to the Absolute as manifested in a woman. The Absolute is also passively receptive because, inasmuch as It appears in the form of a woman, It is under man's control and subject to his orders. Hence to contemplate the Absolute in woman is to see both aspects simultaneously, and such vision is more perfect than seeing It in all the forms in which It manifests Itself. That is why woman is creative, not created. For both qualities, active and passive, belong to the Essence of the Creator, and both are manifested in woman.' (R. Nicholson, *The Mathnawī.*)

Active and passive are essentially equal, and one's preparedness to be awakened, and to begin the journey, depends upon both. Preparedness is the ability to conceive of the possibilities inherent in Being. It is being receptive in order to conceive. This receptiveness is not total passivity but rather 'the power of receiving'. Ibn ʿArabī continues:

'There is no distinction between the two qualities, because the receptivity which is the power to receive is perfectly equal to the power to act, the former being in no way inferior to the latter.' (T. Izutsu.)

They are complements which participate in the gathering together. When the artisan is actively conceiving of the possibilities in the transformation of his clay, the material remains receptive; and yet the clay determines the activity of the artisan.

To return to the analogy of the circle: the circumference is the outer form, which may be either masculine or feminine. The 'process' of reaching centre in either case (the radius) constitutes the feminine principle within all things: it is the soul, the motion, love. The centre itself is the Spirit, the Intellect, the Logos, and is the masculine principle which exists in a state of potentiality within all things and is actualized only in the human form, the place of gathering.

Thus, it is the feminine principle, the soul, which is active, and the masculine principle lies within, as Christ, the Spirit, lay within the Virgin Mary. Transformation takes place when the container is first made ready to receive through spiritual practices, and the possibilities, the preparedness, the Archetypes within, are conceived, develop and grow. After suffering the pains of birth, the Mary within gives birth to the spirit (p. 82). The process is the feminine principle; that which is first born is the masculine. This is why, in spiritual transformation and rebirth, only the masculine principle can be born, for the feminine principle is the process itself. Once birth is given to the spirit, this principle remains as Fatima (p. 83), the Creative Feminine, the daughter of the Prophet, in a state of potentiality within the spirit reborn.

THE QUEST: THE ARC OF ASCENT

Mystic Quest

The process whereby the soul enters the Arc of Ascent and undertakes the mystic Quest lies in the techniques and methods of Sufism, which are centred upon the ability one has to *concentrate*. The object of concentration becomes the Divine and we become Divine-centred. Concentration is a very difficult act: it is harder to give oneself than to give the fruit of one's action. One's urges are stronger towards outwardness, and thus all the methods of Sufism seek the centre. Without the ability to meditate or contemplate, it is impossible to control the urges of the soul. You must seek a certain stillness; you cannot hear the voice of God until you are still.

The method is one of spiritual alchemy. Through transformation, the substance of the soul is changed. The liquid in the cup becomes transparent, so that the container and the contained become one.

There is a saying of the Sufis: 'Knowledge without practice is like a tree without fruit.' Up to this point we have essentially spoken of the process and the doctrine. Now we turn to the method; but it is important to remember that practice is never the same for all people, whereas the doctrine is.

The first step is to seek a Shaykh (pp. 40–41); for although there have been Sufis who have been initiated without a living spiritual master, it is very rare. (Known as *uwaisī*, most of these Sufis have been guided by the Prophet Khizr, who corresponds to the Biblical Elijah.) The purpose of the Shaykh is to cleanse the heart of the disciple so that the disciple may then come to reflect the rays of the beauty of Divine Unity. The awakening begins with expansion, for that is the centrifugal motion away from the contracted ego. (Once awakened and conscious, one must learn a new form of contraction.) The awakening may occur in one of two ways: one either has an extraordinary experience which enables one to overcome one's habits – such as a dream, an illness or a great love – or seeks a spiritual retreat (*khalwat*, pp. 94–95), where one is forced to cut oneself off from everyday experiences. Spiritual practices need the support of external forms – ritual artifacts such as the Quran (p. 52), the place of prayer (p. 53), the mosque (p. 42), the niche (p. 47), and calligraphy (p. 103).

Spiritual Methods

Initiation. In Sufism, initiation (p. 38) symbolizes the death and rebirth of the individual ego. It connects the seeker spiritually to the Infinite; it is the attainment of the covenant with God.

The power to bestow initiation comes from the Prophet. Muḥammad (ﷺ) received, as one of his functions, the power to initiate individuals into the Divine Mysteries, so that mankind could see things in a new way. The various orders of Sufis, each associated with a Saint who received great powers along the spiritual Way, extend to the present through a continuous chain of transmission which goes back to the time of the Prophet. This chain of transmission is the only guarantee of the authenticity and regularity of the spiritual Presence. The Presence must come from God, and begins with revelation; initiation is a means of opening the door. Going in depends upon one's will.

Meditation. The function of meditation is to prevent the mind from going astray while the heart concentrates on God. The psyche is like a battlefield, or like the sea which never ceases creating waves. It has to be stilled and made to look inward.

Invocation. In Sufism, meditation (*fikr*) is the passive counterpart of active invocation (*zikr*). The human form cannot cease to think, but it can transcend thought. In activities such as the making of music, chanting and the spiritual dance (pp. 90–91), the resistance of the restless psyche is gradually worn down, and the body becomes the temple of God, empty of self and filled with Self.

However, one cannot transcend will through an act of will; and there is no meditation possible without an invocation, a Name of God, given through a spiritual master who carries the chain of transmission. This brings the Divine Presence into the sound. Human speech is in a special relationship to the soul: we are restored to our original state, as we were created, through the Divine Word. God's invocation of us is the whole of existence.

The word *zikr*, invocation, has really three meanings: to mention, to invoke, to remember. When we mention God, we invoke His Name; when we invoke His Name, we remember Him. The symbolism of this is a mystery. God is present in His Names because of His love for us.

Within invocation there is a pattern of meditation, which varies according to the master and the order. The fibre of the universe is the word breathed through the Breath of the Compassionate. By invoking God, we give our existence back to Him. There is a Divine Substance in the air, and God takes our breath and light and integrates it into His being. Most people do it unconsciously. If we can become aware of our breathing and the spiritual substance of the breath, then we gain the spiritual energy that resides in the air.

As a bridge between the daily prayers and the invocation, the Sufi begins by performing the *wird* or litany. Every order chooses a verse of the Quran or a prayer of the Prophet which is repeated a certain number of times: it is, in a sense, a magical formula peculiar to the order. In the *wird* there are three stages: purification (death), expansion (love) and union with God. The repetition continues, either alone or in assembly, aloud or silently, until the Sufi identifies the heartbeat with the Divine Presence.

Contemplation. In contemplation (*shuhūd*), one concentrates on a visual image or on an idea which must have a Divine Quality, that is, one of the positive qualities in the cosmos such as the virtues of charity, humility and truthfulness. One either isolates this in the mind or puts it in a formula. The contemplation is often performed with bodily motion, so that the soul may dissociate itself from the body.

Spiritual Virtues

There are three basic spiritual virtues, stemming from the Quran, which the Sufi internalizes. The three are humility (*khushūʻ*), charity (*karāmat*) and truthfulness (*ṣidq*).

The first, humility, corresponds to one's being and not to one's actions. It is the realization that God is everything and we are nothing. All manifestation returns whence it has come. Ibn ʻArabī said that humility is too profound a virtue for God to have given it to any creature fully. Essentially, it is awareness of two things: first, that, we are non-existent, for actually only God exists; and second, that every human being has something to teach us, because, although the human form is limited, the limitations are never the same in two different people.

Charity is a virtue very closely connected to nobility. At the highest level it is giving self to God, and therefore the supreme charity is to invoke the Name of God. Charity is to realize that we have nothing; everything comes from and belongs to God.

Truthfulness lifts us from the plane of existence to the plane of knowledge. It is to see things in their transparent state: to see things as they really are.

The three virtues are internalized when we see the universe as symbolic of the Divine Presence; once internalized, and reflected in the form, the virtues lead us to spiritual union with the Source from which we came.

SYMBOLISM

It is through symbols that one is awakened; it is through symbols that one is transformed; and it is through symbols that one expresses. Symbols are realities contained within the nature of things. The entire journey in God is a journey in symbols, in which one is constantly aware of the higher reality within things. Symbols reflect both Divine transcendence and Divine immanence; they refer to both the universal aspect of *creation* and the particular aspect of *tradition*.

Symbolism is perhaps the most sacred of Sufi sciences, for it is through seeing symbols that one continues to remember, to invoke. Each time one forgets, and is pulled back into the sea of the unconscious psychic forces, one must struggle again to remember; and it is only through an understanding of the symbolic that one can do so.

Symbols are vehicles of transmission of Divine realities, which transform us by carrying us to the higher states of being from which they originate. Known as a world unto themselves (*ʻālam-i-mithāl*), they are the place of encounter between the world of Archetypes or intelligibles and the sensible, phenomenal world. The world of symbols is a reflection of the world of Archetypes. It gathers these universal essences and then reflects them down upon this world. The further a thing moves away from the intelligible world of illuminated knowledge, and the closer to the sensible world of phenomena, the more particularity it outwardly exhibits. Its universal essence moves inward, into a state of potentiality.

Everything in creation is a symbol: for everything perceived by the *outer* senses may be conceived through the *inner* senses as a sign of a higher state of reality. However, this symbolic vision takes place, for the Sufi,. only when the symbol is seen in the presence of the theophanic light. This light is the knowledge of illumination, which arises after the mystic has passed through the Divine Law, gained the Knowledge of Certainty through knowledge of the doctrines of Sufism, seen through the inner meaning of practices and rites with the Eye of Certainty, and reached the centre to gain the Truth of Certainty. This theophanic light is not seen; it is that which makes one see as it makes itself seen in the form through which it shines.

As to the attitude of the individual creator who gives the symbol its concrete form, it may be a completely unconscious one, in which case one could call it *participation mystique*: oneness with nature. Tradition, for such a creator, has ensured that there has been no separation from the sacred, from the Divine order. The expression is one with the image created. The creator has never been separated actively from the tradition, and rites and practices allow a rhythmic and harmonic transformation which flows into the form created.

Alternatively, the artist's image may be an extension of a super-conscious attitude. In this case, there has been a break with primordial nature: a stepping-aside, an objective reflection of the natural processes. This may be termed a spiritual awakening. The next step is the retracing of the steps, descending back to the point where one was at one with nature. By doing so, one unveils one's ego-oriented attitudes, and each unveiling removes a darkness which allows more light to shine through. After this process, one rebuilds the container, through rites and practices particular to the tradition to which one has been awakened. One is inspired by universal forms, but inspiration finds expression only in one's particular tradition.

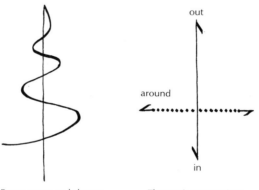

Permanence and change   Three primary motions

A tradition is a Divine norm which maintains the permanence and continuity of the particular people who hold it. It relates the whole of life to certain principles which transcend the human plane. It repeats, recalls, recollects the Divine Ideas or Archetypes. It is religion in its most universal aspect. In its aspect of continuity or permanence, it continues a chain of oral transmission which relates it through the Vertical Cause to the Source from which all things emanated. Continuity is not simply a horizontal line of human history. Continuity pierces the horizontal line with the vertical axis of revelation, and thereby relates the tradition to a transhistorical time. It is tradition, sanctified by revelation, which creates and preserves the universe of forms, ideas and institutions. The forms appear in art and in the crafts; the ideas are reflected, expressed and recalled in the intellectual development of each tradition; and its institutions retain the forms and ideas for future generations. However a symbol has been expressed, the Sufi knows that 'man cannot create symbols: he is transformed by them'.

To describe or organize or categorize symbols will not exhaust them, for they exist whether or not one refers to them. The process is far more complex than this; for if one remains at this level of description, one becomes absorbed in immanence, which is only one aspect of the Divine. At the same time as one comes to know immanence, one must come to know transcendence, for only then is a transformation possible; and the goal of the Quest is transformation.

Universal and Particular Symbols

There is an essential division in the science of symbolism. Universal (or natural) symbols are symbols as they appear in the nature of things. They are primordial to mankind, and in this sense they are trans-cultural. Particular symbols, or even particular interpretations of universal symbols, differ according to the various traditions. They are sensible or intelligible forms consecrated by God through revelation to become vehicles of Divine Grace. They possess, in a sense, the theophanic light which confers a dimension of transcendence on the particular tradition in which they are revealed.

In Sufism, universal metaphysical symbols – expressed particularly in architecture, music and calligraphy – stem from the Quran, the Word; and the Word contains the Names and Qualities. Symbols connected to sound, light and the Intellect are among the most profound expressions in Sufism. The Word is both a sound and a light, for the light is the meaning of the Word. The Word is as a mirror where the Divine reverberates outwardly. It is through sound that the world will be re-absorbed at the Day of Judgment. The niche (*miḥrāb*, p. 47), which directs one towards Mecca and towards the Kaʿbah (p. 46), and the porch (*īwān*, p. 79), which waits patiently to catch the light, symbolize the Presence of the Divine Name *Nūr*, Light.

Particular symbols may be divided into many categories, according to the means of expression. There are cosmological (pp. 56–57) and psychological (pp. 68–71) symbols, and symbols of revelation (pp. 72–83), as well as particular interpretations of universal symbols. Each one of these areas in Sufism is traditionally a science based on the Quran and interpreted through *taʿwīl*, the art of spiritual hermeneutics.

The best example of a good word, ʿAbū Bakr Sirāj al-Dīn tells us, 'is a Divine Name, recalled, remembered, invoked in an upward aspiration towards the Truth. The firm set root of the tree is the [*zikr*, invocation], itself uttered with firm set purpose. The Heaven-reaching branches represent the tremendous import of the [invocation] as it passes upwards throughout the whole of the universe; and the fruit of the tree is the Reality in whose remembrance the invocation is performed.'

As to cosmological symbols, the cosmic mountain, Qāf, refers to the renewal of the world, the rejuvenation of the cosmos (p. 56). The mountain symbolizes the infinite expanse of the sky, the single and highest point in space. It is the Source of the whole of the cosmos, and yet only a point in the Divine Infinity. As one descends towards the lower states of being, the horizontal dimension expands. The further from origin one is, the more one has a sense of expansion; but one is moving away from the centre.

Mountain climbing corresponds to the inner aspects of life. The Divine Law is the horizontal base. One needs a guide to climb: one can climb a mountain by many paths, but one needs to follow one made by experienced people. The higher one climbs, the

*Hast thou not seen how God citeth a symbol? 'A good word
is as a good tree –
its root set firm,
and its branches in heaven;
giving its fruit at every season
by the leave of its Lord.'
So God citeth symbols for men
that they may remember.*

Quran 14:29–31,
trans. A. J. Arberry

smaller things below become, but the further one can see. The higher one moves spiritually, the more vision one gains. Only at the peak can one see the other peaks.

The mountain has trees and plants and is full of natural forms; then one passes the tree-line and enters the world without forms. One passes from form to formlessness, from sensible to intelligible. The name of the person who reaches the top of the cosmic mountain is Simurgh (p. 36).

The Pen and the Guarded Tablet are also cosmological symbols. From the ink of Divine Knowledge God wrote the essential existence of all things through the Pen, the masculine principle operative in creation; existent things are words inscribed upon the Guarded Tablet, the Universal Soul or feminine principle operative in the universe. The Pen and the Guarded Tablet stem from the Tradition: 'If all the oceans were turned to ink, one would still not be able to describe all the Qualities of God.' Another Tradition which refers to them is: 'God wrote the Quran upon the Tablet. The first drop of ink was the dot under the letter *b* which begins *Bismi 'Llah* . . . [In the Name of God. . . . p. 55].' The Pen produces the point; the point is the centre; the centre is the Divine Source.

One of the most beautiful of all symbols, which has found unexcelled expression in Islamic architecture, carpet design and poetry, is that of the Gardens of Paradise. Paradise is described in the Quran (55:45–75) as being four gardens. These are interpreted esoterically as four stages through which the mystic travels on the inward journey. The four gardens are called the Garden of the Soul, the Garden of the Heart, the Garden of the Spirit, and the Garden of Essence.

As the mystic begins the ascent through the Gardens of Paradise, the point of encounter is the Garden of the Soul. This is the feminine principle within, structured by gateways of sense. In order to enter, the mystic must gather together the inner senses or faculties of intuition. The object sought by these faculties is the spiritual Heart, which is the abode of intuition. The mystic encounters perils in entering this garden, as the soul is pulled away from centre by physical desires. The mystic is in a state of receptivity, with a readiness to be satisfied; but if the soul is actually satisfied, the mystic is expelled from the garden much as Adam was expelled from Eden.

The mystic perseveres and steps beyond the gateway into the Garden of the Soul proper. The garden contains three things: a fountain, flowing water and the fruit of trees. The fountain symbolizes perceptions of particulars: forms and ideas. Having reached this fountain, the mystic gains Knowledge of Certainty.

The water which is found here symbolizes Light: knowledge which gushes from the Fountain of the Spirit, flows to the Garden of the Heart, and from there feeds the faculties of intuition which are partially veiled by psychic forces here in the Garden of the Soul.

The waters give full flavour to the fruits grown from trees (thoughts) of meditation. Particular objects of perception are no longer outward-directed: the mystic, in a sense, seals the gateways and then in the Garden of the Soul, through meditation, is able to refer the particular objects of perception beyond their particular meaning to their Archetypes in the Garden of the Heart. The mystic makes use of the thinking function in its highest form.

The mystic knows further that even the Archetypes are but shadows of higher realities. The Archetypes, as universal forms, flow to the Garden of the Soul and to its fountain or source which then feeds its fruit.

But such as fears the Station of his Lord,
for them shall be two gardens –
O which of your Lord's bounties
will you and you deny?...
therein two fountains of running water –
O which of your Lord's bounties
will you and you deny?
therein of every fruit two kinds –
O which of your Lord's bounties
will you and you deny?...
And besides these shall be two gardens –
O which of your Lord's bounties
will you and you deny?
green, green pastures –
O which of your Lord's bounties
will you and you deny?
therein two fountains of gushing water –
O which of your Lord's bounties
will you and you deny?
therein fruit
and the date palm, and the pomegranates –
O which of your Lord's bounties
will you and you deny?

Quran 55:46–66,
trans. A. J. Arberry

The mystic then turns towards the next garden, the Garden of the Heart. These two gardens, that of the Soul and that of the Heart, together symbolize the totality of the perfection of human nature.

The Garden of the Heart is structured by the feminine principle's spiritual becoming. It is the abode of intuition, ruled by the spiritual Heart or Active Intellect, known traditionally as the instrument of gnosis, or illuminated knowledge. To enter, the mystic must leave reason behind.

As the mystic enters this second garden, further perils present themselves. Until the mystic reaches the fountain of this garden and eats of the fruit of the tree, there is a danger of falling, due to the potency of psychic forces.

The mystic enters the garden and finds a fountain, water which flows, a tree and fruit of this tree. The fountain is the Fountain of Life or Immortality. By drinking of this fountain, the mystic attains to the Eye of Certainty, that is, reaches direct contact with the Spirit; for the water of this fountain originates from the Garden of the Spirit.

The water which flows in this garden is the Intellect, knowledge which has been illuminated by revelation. Having left reason behind, which relates to the sensible world, the mystic's soul is fed by the Intellect which rules the intelligible or spiritual world.

The tree in this garden is the Tree of Life or Immortality: its fruits are universal meanings which relate all forms and images to the inner sameness existing within all things. Universal meanings may be taken by the mystic, however, only when there has been a phenomenal image, an imprint upon the soul.

Having gathered particular and universal meanings from these first two gardens, the mystic moves inward to the Garden of the Spirit. This garden is structured by a higher and a lower part. The lower part contains the seven Prophets of one's being, one's seven subtle forms which correspond in the macrocosm to the seven visible planets (see p. 97). At the division between the lower and upper parts of the Garden is the flowering of the Tree of Knowledge. Its roots are in the lower part, but its fruit grows in the upper regions. The higher part of this garden is known as the Garden of Refuge. Here, structurally, the feminine principle is reaching towards completion in the masculine principle.

To enter this Garden of the Spirit, the mystic's preparedness or potentiality has been reabsorbed in primordial nature. The mystic is on the verge of union with the Secret, the spiritual centre or mystery within.

Perils still present themselves. The mystic is reabsorbed in the light of Muḥammad (ص), the Logos, the Spirit, which was 'when Adam was between water and clay'. At this point, the mystic sees with the eye of this light and sees all lights unveiled. If not fully prepared, the mystic slips back to ordinary vision and loses the direct contact with the Spirit.

The mystic enters the Garden of the Spirit and finds a fountain, water which gushes forth, a tree and fruit of that tree. The fountain is the Fountain of Knowledge which is illuminated by the Spirit. It is the contemplative Truth of Certainty, the knowledge of Illumination, knowledge of the Oneness of all Divine Qualities. The Fountain of Knowledge appears like veils of light, not darkness, behind each of which shines the Light of Essence Itself. The water in this garden gushes forth of Itself; it is like the oil in the Verse of Light which burns 'though no fire touched it'.

The Tree of Knowledge grows next to the fountain; it stretches itself to the uppermost boundaries of the Spirit. The fruit of this garden is the date from which the Virgin Mary nourished herself after giving birth to the Spirit. This fruit symbolizes contemplation of Divine Light and the appearance of Divine Majesty and Beauty. It is the fruit of the station of the Spirit, where only a kernel of individuality of the mystic remains; in this garden the kernel receives nourishment and delights from the fruit of contemplation.

Finally, the mystic enters the Garden of Essence. Its form consists of the masculine and feminine principles uniting in the stage of annihilation, being reborn in the illuminated knowledge of the Unity of Being.

To enter, the mystic must lose all traces of individuality. The Divine Self can now see Self reflected in the 'polished' mirror of the Sufi, empty of human self. The only peril in this garden is to the mystic's individuality, for it dies a spiritual death.

Upon entering this Garden, the mystic finds the Fountain of Knowledge of the Unity of Being; the water which gushes forth is pure Light. The fruit of this Garden is the pomegranate, the symbol of integration of multiplicity in unity, in the station of Union, conscious of Essence. Consumed in the Light, no individuality remains; the mystic has reached the goal of the Quest, the Truth of Certainty.

Now the mystic redescends through the Arc of Descent back to the phenomenal world in a state of subsistence. Seeing the gardens in reverse order, the mystic completes the circle in knowing the Garden of Essence as Light, where the Knowledge of Unity gushes forth; the Garden of the Spirit, symbolized by the sun, where Knowledge of the Oneness of all Divine Qualities gushes forth of Itself; the Garden of the Heart, whose waters flow from the Intellect and whose Fountain of Life is fed by the Fountain of the Spirit as the moon receives the light of the sun; and finally the Garden of the Soul. The Garden of the Soul is as moonlight, reflecting the Unity of Being, the Spirit and universal meanings into all particular forms. Subsisting through God, the mystic, now Sufi, has returned from the Quest.

Part 2
The 'What' of Mystical Expression

THE JOURNEY TO GOD

The Awakening

The journey to God begins with an awakening to the concept that the phenomenal world is a veil which conceals the Divine. We begin the Quest by removing the veil, only to become aware that the veil and the Divine are one and the same thing. The veil is the theophany itself: the manifestation of the Divine through Its Names and Qualities. When we see the veil, we are seeing nothing but the Divine. (Inside the Shaykh Luṭfullāh Mosque, Isfahān, Iran, 17th c.)

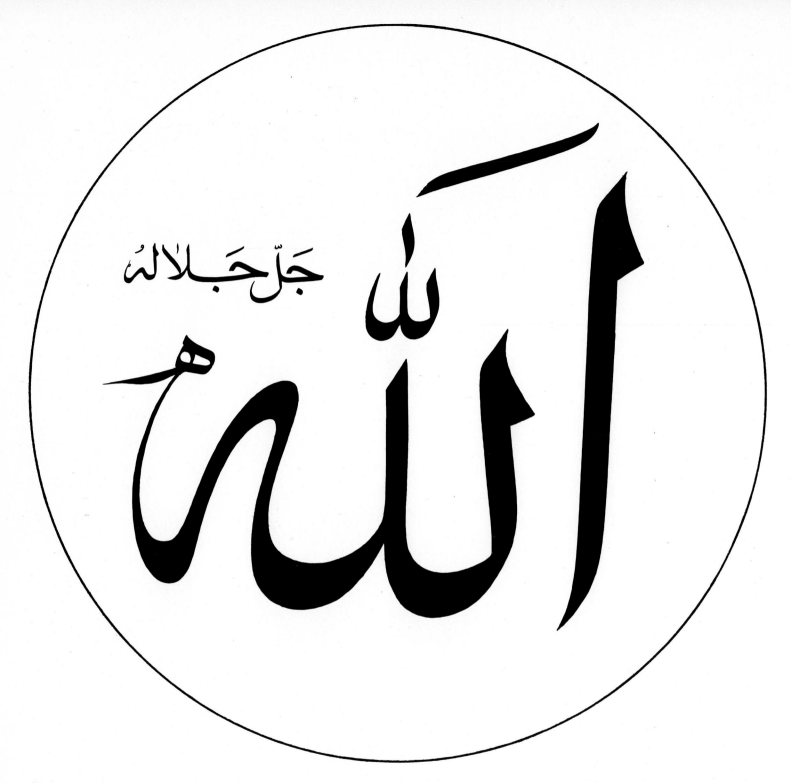

The Call

The awakening of consciousness is activated by intuitive perception of the symbolic meaning of the two testimonies whereby one declares oneself to be a Muslim. The first, 'There is no god but God', discloses the Name (*Allāh*) by which one first comes to know the Divine. One who comes to know the Divine is described as 'one whose heart and purpose are drowned in God, so as to see nothing but Him'. The second testimony is 'Muḥammad is the Prophet of God'. To the Sufi, Muḥammad (ص) is the Universal Prototype (see p. 10): the

place of gathering of all possibilities. The emulation of the Prophet, aided by Divine Grace, allows the transformation of the mystic into a similar reservoir of possibilities. The word Muhammad means 'the one praised'. (Calligraphies of 'God, Glory be to His Majesty', *Allāh Jall Jalālhū*, and 'Muḥammad is the Prophet of God, *Muḥammad rasula ʿLlah,* by Jalil Rassouli, after Hagia Sophia Mosque; Istanbul.)

The Gathering

The gathering begins at the level of the spiritual faculties of intuition. These are symbolized by the birds, whose language is the language of self and contains know-ledge of the higher states of being: 'And Solomon was David's heir, and he said, "O men, we have been taught the language of the birds, and all favours have been showered upon us"' (Quran 27 : 15). This language of the birds in the human world is rhythmic language, and the science of

rhythm (see p. 110) is the means by which one reaches the higher states of being.

In the story of *The Conference of the Birds*, by the twelfth-century Persian poet 'Aṭṭār, the hoopoe (left), the symbol of inspiration, assembles the birds (or faculties) to begin the Quest for the fabulous Simurgh. Those who are attached to the phenomenal world give excuses for not making the journey. The nightingale, that aspect of self caught in the exterior form of things, cannot leave the rose: the duck cannot leave the water; the hawk cannot

leave its prey. Only those faculties which have been awakened to the inner aspect of things, and see beyond materiality, choose to make the journey towards completion.

At the end of the Quest, the birds find that the Simurgh (above) has been with them, guiding them from within, through-out the journey. The goal of the Quest is the Self. (The Conference of the Birds, details from ms. of *Mantiq al-Tayr*, by Farīd al-Dīn 'Aṭṭār, miniatures by Ḥabīb Allāh, Iran, 17th c.; the Simurgh, detail from ms. of *Shah Nameh*, by Firdawsi, Iran, 17th c.)

Initiation and Invocation

the giving of the outward symbols of the order. These allow the initiate to know aspects of self as reflected in external forms. The bowl (*kashkūl*) symbolizes the individual's passive, receptive nature. The double axe (*tabar*) symbolizes the individual's active nature as agent. The animal skin (*pūstīn*) serves the purpose of orientation in two ways: first, it is upon this place that one sits and meditates; second, it is to this space that one relates one's possessions. To own more than would fit upon this skin, or more than would fit in one's *chantah* or rug bag, is to have reached the state of forgetfulness.

The names of God which are recited by the various orders, and included in their invocation, are the means by which the soul passes from stage to stage in its journey. The Names invoked vary among the orders, but they are usually seven in number. A branch of the Khalwatī Order invokes the first testimony as the first Name, and six other Names. *Lā ilāha illa'Llah,* 'There is no god but God', is repeated 100,000 times, when the animal soul (Quran 12 : 53) prevails, before the initiate is prepared to be given the second. The Shaykh then breathes the second Name, *Allāh*, God, into the ear of the initiate, whose soul comes to know its own imperfections (Quran 75 : 2). Third is, *Hū*, He, the stage of the inspired soul (Quran 91 : 7–8). The fifth Name given by the Shaykh is *Ḥayy*; this Name symbolizes the contented soul. The sixth Name, *Qayyūm*, the Eternal, is the journey of the satisfied soul. The seventh and final Name breathed into the ear of the mystic by this order is *Qahhār*, the Subduer. This Name symbolizes the stage of the perfected soul, journeying from the world of Unity back to multiplicity through subsistence (*baqā'*). (Carpet of Sufi Darvish symbols; the Seven Names invoked by the Khalwatī initiate under the direction of the Shaykh, calligraphy by Jalil Rassouli.)

Through initiation, following the example of the Prophet as related in the Quran, 'God was well pleased with the believers [the Companions of the Prophet] when they swore allegiance beneath the tree' (48 : 18), the Shaykh re-enacts the covenant between man and the Divine Presence in

The Guide

As one can be activated only through a form outside one's self, it is necessary to seek out a living spiritual master as a guide in the journey to God.

The Divine Name *Hādī,* Guide, contains two aspects. The first, known as *takwīnī,* is universal; it exists within creation. Whatever is created is naturally, through an unconscious process, shown the Way of the return: 'He is the One who gave unto everything its nature, then guided it aright' (20 : 50). Ghazālī expands this aspect of *Hādī:* 'He guides the young bird to pick up seeds from the time of its hatching; He guides the bee to building its house in a hexagonal form. . . .', for to worship, to give praise, is inborn.

The second aspect of guidance, *tashrī'ī,* the guidance that comes from Revelation, is more particular, in the sense that it relates to the consciousness of the human form; for it is through *tashrī'ī* that God sends Prophets and Divine Law. Only guidance through the Divine Law shows one what to worship, what should be praised. The role of the spiritual master in Sufism, who continues to reflect the Divine Grace bestowed upon the Prophet, is to guide the initiate through Divine Revelation towards the straight path in the journey to God. (Carpet depicting Nūr ʿAlī Shāh, 19th-c. Shaykh of the Niʿmatullāhī Order: painting of Hajjī Bektāshī, 13th-c. founder of the Bektāshī Order.)

The Gateway and The Bridge

Through initiation one enters a gateway and sets out across a bridge. The gateway, in architecture, expresses movement through defined space. The implied sense of passage that the gateway brings is a necessary first step of the journey. The bridge symbolizes the human being as mediator between heaven and earth, as container of both human and divine nature; and it relates to the role of mankind both as the vice-regent of God on earth, responsible for preserving nature, and as the servant of God, acting out His will. On the spiritual journey these two concepts must be bridged, so that one retains the balance of one's own nature while at the same time realizing that all is God. (Gateway to the Shaykh Luṭfullāh Mosque, Isfahān, Iran, 17th c.; Khwājū bridge, Isfahān, Iran, 16th c.)

Perils

Entering the gateway in the journey to God brings one into a dichotomous situation. One has embarked upon the Way; but one's psyche has been opened to all the perils that the journey offers. These perils are often described in traditional myths as the demons (jinn) or as the dragon.

The jinn, or psychic forces of nature, appear as both sensible and intelligible substances. While mankind is created of clay, and angels of light, the jinn originally appeared as smokeless vapours. Jinn are both the hostile forces in nature, still not subdued by man, and the means whereby one achieves salvation. Jinn may be of either sex, and they live collectively with a leader. All their activities take place at night, and it is the jinn who inflict illnesses both physical and psychic. One is admonished to pass by quickly, or they will delay the journey.

In astronomy, the dragon relates to the nodes, two diametrically opposed points of intersection between the paths of the moon and the sun. Its head is the ascending node, its tail the descending node. An eclipse can occur only when both sun and moon stand at the nodes. To the mystic, the dragon symbolizes the place of encounter between the moon and sun within (see pp. 60–61). The dragon can either devour the moon, seen symbolically as the mystic's spiritual Heart, or it can serve as the place or container of conception. By entering the dragon when the sun is in the nodes, the moon or Heart conceives. Thus, in full consciousness of the perils, one must enter the dragon in order to await the eclipse in its cosmic womb. (Tahmuras defeating the jinn; Esfandiyar killing the dragon; details from ms. of *Shah Nameh*, by Firdawsi, Iran, 17th c.)

Orientation

One of the most important rites of Sufism is that of orientation, in particular to the Centre to which one orients one's daily prayers, the Ka'bah. To the Sufi it symbolizes the Divine Essence, while the Black Stone within it symbolizes the human spiritual essence. The pilgrim circumambulates it seven times in two rhythmic patterns, and thereby, essentially, spirals around the terrestrial centre which is none other than the Vertical Cause, the Divine and cosmic axis.

The niche, *mihrab*, in a mosque is oriented towards the Ka'bah, and it is the place where the leader in prayer stands and recites the daily prayers. The niche reflects his incantations of the Divine Word to the congregation, who then repeat the words after him. The Divine words which reverberate from the niche are symbols of the Presence of God. It is this that evokes in the Sufi his motivation towards prayer, for the miracle of Islam is the direct transformation of the Divine Word, in the Quran, by ritual recitation and invocation. (The Ka'bah, Mecca: the *mihrab* in the Shaykh Luṭfullāh Mosque, Isfahān, Iran, 17th c.)

When a rite is performed without knowledge of its symbolism, its metaphysical quality remains hidden, inactive. This is particularly true of the rite of ablution. Water is the medium of the ablution inseparable from Muslim prayer; but in itself it is only the symbol of the purifying Absolute Water, the pure spring of the Spirit which flows in the heart of the transformed mystic, and which in a true sense is the Fountain of Life.

Traditionally, the place of kindred souls of the spirit is the *khānaqāh*, an earthly Paradise, a space filled by the unrestrained poems and songs of the Sufi. Shihāb al-Dīn Yaḥya Suhrawardī describes the brotherhood: 'Do not withhold words from the fit. The unfit themselves, from the words of the people of truth, become weary. . . . The heart of the unfit and strangers towards truth is like the wick of a lamp which has been filled with water rather than oil. No matter how many times you light it, it will not light. But the heart of a friend is like an oil lamp which draws and mixes fire from a distance.' (Fountain in the Garden of Fīn, Kāshān, Iran, 16th c.; The Ni ʿmatullāhī Khānaqāh, Māhān, Iran, 15th c.)

The motions of the body in the daily prayers
– standing, bending and prostration – imitate exactly the ascending, descending and
horizontal motions of the Spirit in creating
the world, that is, in manifesting Self. Ritual
prayer, in repeating these gestures, re-
enacts the Creation. The prayer of God is
His aspiration to manifest Self, to see Self in
a mirror, but particularly in a mirror which
itself sees Him. This mirror can only be the
faithful, whose Lord He is, and in whom He
invests one of His Names. The rite of prayer
fulfils this Divine aspiration by becoming
the mirror of the Face whereby the Sufi, in
prayer, comes to see the 'Face of God' in
the most sacred niche of self. But the Sufi
would never see the Face of God if his
vision were not itself the prayer of God.

Daily prayers are performed upon prayer
carpets whose pattern incorporates a niche.
The niche may hold a lamp or, as in the
sevenfold family prayer carpet here, it may
hold the cosmic tree. (Multiple prayer carpet, Samarkand, 19th c.; Shrine of Shah
Zadeh Huseyn, Qasvin, Iran, 19th c.)

The Sufi orients self, in particular, to the Quran. Revealed to the Prophet while he was in an unlettered or virgin state, it is the very substance of God; and all of Sufism can be traced to it. It literally means 'recitation', and it calls out to the Sufi to return through the Word as it was revealed to Muḥammad (ﷺ). It has been expressed in many art forms, but, in particular, in calligraphy. Its most important role to the Sufi is as the source of remembrance and evocation.

Finally, the orientation is towards emptiness and total receptivity: spiritual death. One of the most famous sayings of the Prophet is 'Die before you die.' The tomb room in Konya of Jalāl al-Dīn Rūmī, the founder of the Maulawī Order, is actually the place of his wedding; for the night of his death is celebrated with all the joy that surrounds a wedding. It is through death that he is finally united with his Beloved. (Page of ms. of Quran, Iran, 16th c.; tomb room of Maulawī Order, Konya, Turkey, 13th c.)

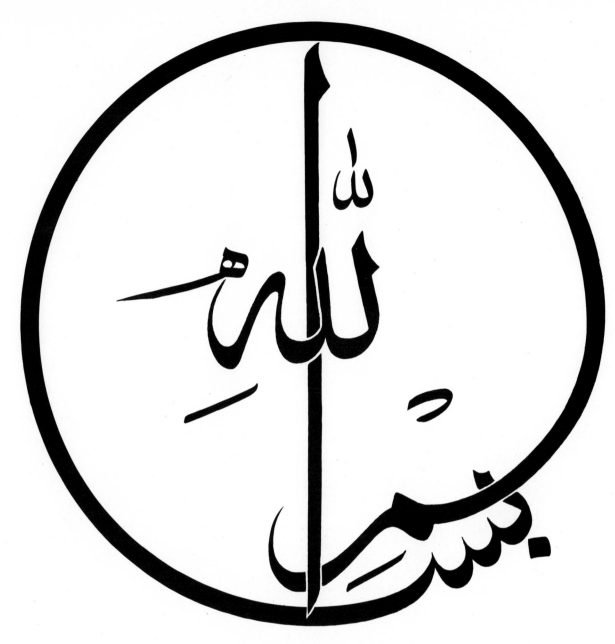

THE JOURNEY IN GOD

In the Name of God

The chapters of the Quran begin with: 'In the Name of God, the Compassionate, the Merciful'. In a sense, all of Sufism is contained in these words. All things are created in the Name of God. The Name *Allāh* contains all the Names, and every mystic returns through one of them. But a Name is not only *what* the mystic expresses: the process of invocation itself – the *why* and *how* of expression – constitutes the Breath

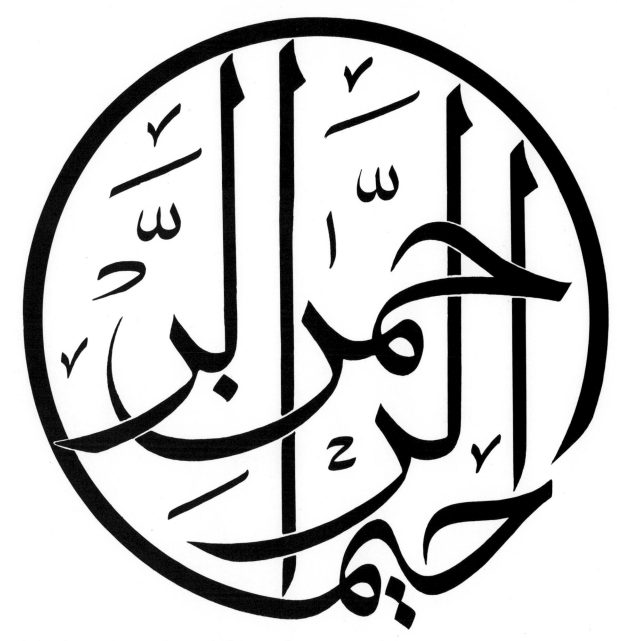

of the Spirit, which is the Divine Name *Raḥmān*, the Compassionate: 'God taught the Quran through the Compassionate' (55 : 1). The Compassionate is the Divine Breath which breathes life into all forms. The mystic mirrors this process through the process of invoking a Name.

The mystic now journeys in God, conscious of the Divine Presence in all forms and simultaneously aware of the Divine Reality which transcends all forms. This is essentially a journey in symbols, forms which serve as the transmutative force as the mystic moves closer to God.

Every symbol has many facets and levels of interpretation. One approach to their understanding is to begin with the cosmological symbols (pp. 56–67) and their corresponding psychological symbols (pp. 68–71), and finally view religious symbolism, both universal and particular, in the context of Sufism (pp. 72–92). (Calligraphies of 'In the Name of God', and 'The Compassionate, the Merciful', by Jalil Rassouli.)

Cosmological Symbols

The inner symbol of the cosmic mountain, Qāf, has been expressed in the following way: 'What separates man from divine Reality is the slightest of barriers. God is infinitely close to man, but man is infinitely far from God. This barrier, for man, is a mountain . . ., which he must remove with his own hands. He digs away the earth, but in vain, the mountain remains; man however goes on digging in the Name of God. And the mountain vanishes. It was never there.' (F. Schuon, *Stations of Wisdom.*)

The Cosmic Tree, Tuba, in its macrocosmic form grows at the uppermost limits of the universe. In its microcosmic form, its cultivation depends upon the mystic. In a tradition of the Prophet, it is related that 'the Tuba is a tree in Paradise. God planted it with His own hand and breathed His Spirit into it'.

Ibn ʿArabī describes this symbol in both its forms. In its macrocosmic aspect, it is associated with the Cosmic Mountain on top of which the Cosmic Tree grows. The whole of the cosmos is seen as a tree, the Tree of Knowledge, which has grown from the seed of the Divine Command, 'Be!' (see p. 13). The Tree has sent down its roots, sent up its trunk, and spread out its branches, so that this world, the world of Symbols, and the world of Archetypes, are all contained by this Tree.

As it is manifest in a macrocosmic aspect, so it is hidden in the microcosmic form. It is the symbol of wisdom which, through roots in meditation, bears fruit of the Spirit. (Cosmic Mountain, from ms. anthology of Persian poems, Behbahan, Fars, Iran, 14th c.; flannel appliqué work, Isfahān, Iran, 18th c.)

The symbolism of geometric patterns is generated from the number one through the concept of symmetry. Correspondence in size, shape and relative position of the parts to the whole is their ordering principle. Bilateral symmetry is that of a form divisible into two similar halves by either of two planes passing at right angles to each other; radial symmetry is divisible into equal symmetrical portions by any of three or more planes passing through the axis; both symbolize the cosmic processes characterized by extension in all directions, by boundlessness and by infinite divisibility. (Detail of the portal sanctuary of the Friday Mosque, Varamin, Iran, 14th c.; tiles, Morocco, 16th c.)

Overleaf

The sun which lights the day is the symbol of the Spirit which lights the next world; the moon symbolizes the Universal Prototype who is the light of this world. Light is a manifestation of Divine Knowledge; and so, when these cosmological symbols are transferred to the microcosmic plane, the soul of the mystic is symbolized by the moon which reflects the light of the sun. The ray of light which passes between them is the symbol of the Intellect, and that light which is reflected by the moon symbolizes the spiritual intuitions of the mystic: 'Just as the rays of moonlight strike upon various material objects which reflect them according to their aptitude, so the intuitions strike upon the faculties of the mind, which if they have duly received the doctrine will flash back a light of recognition; and this light means that a purely mental understanding of doctrinal teaching has been transferred into the Knowledge of Certainty.' (Abū Bakr Sirāj al-Dīn.) (Purse with sun motif, Iran, 20th c.; Chamber of Salutations, Shrine of Imām Reza, Mashhad, Iran, begun 13th c.)

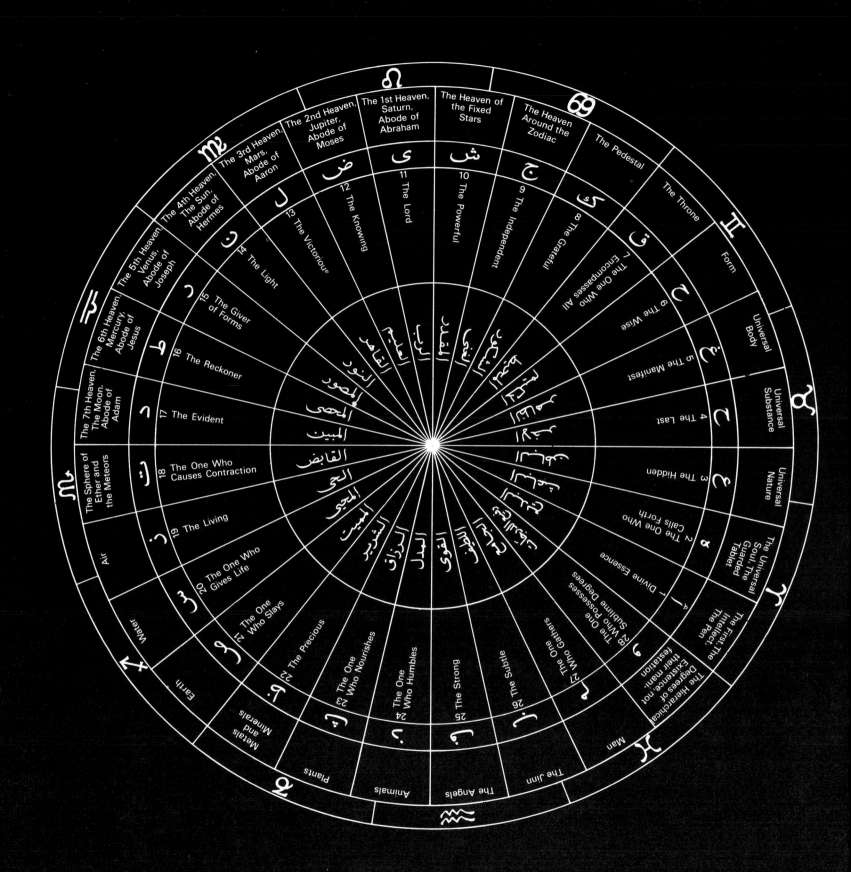

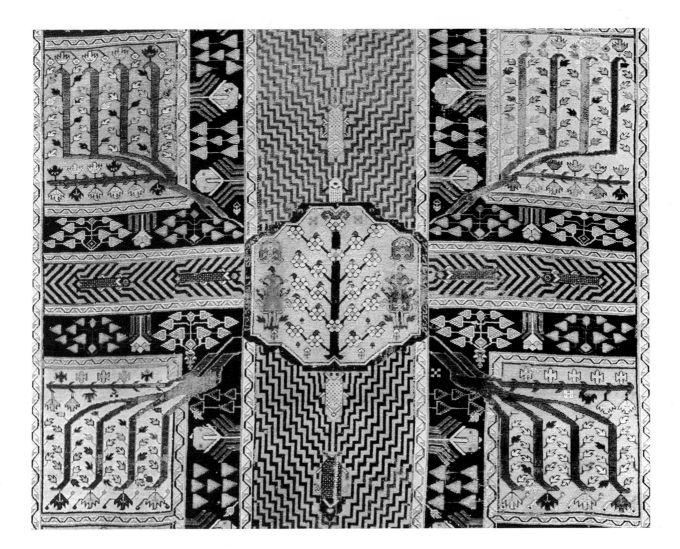

Ibn ʿArabī's chart of creation draws on the correspondences between twenty-eight of the Divine Names and the twenty-eight stations of the moon, each of which corresponds to a letter of the Arabic alphabet. Each letter is a symbol of a particular manifestation, and the entire alphabet sets out the order in which the world was created. All this revolves within the zodiac, by which the sun's motion is measured.

It is through the consciousness of the cosmic axis or Vertical Cause that the Sufi gains a sense of eternity: the permanence of the Identity of Being throughout all the multiplicity of modes and aspects of existence. Awareness, at this supra-rational level, occurs at the very centre of the human state as well as at the centre of all other states. Through intuitive perception of the laws of harmony, which unite all things in the universe, one comes to know the transcendent, formless, unindividualized element of the Vertical Cause. (Chart of Creation, after Titus Burckhardt, *Clé spirituelle de l'astrologie musulmane d'après Moyyiddin Ibn ʿArabī*; detail of garden carpet, Iran, c. 1700.)

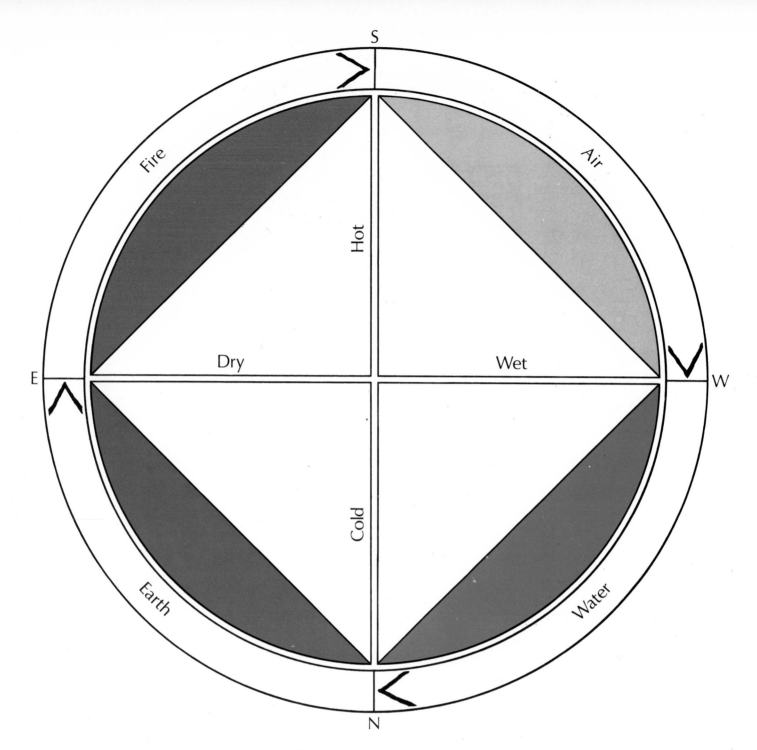

The system of four colours establishes sensible correspondences between what is seen and the various aspects of the inherent energy of nature, which is continuously in search of the order and harmony of its primordial state. This inherent energy manifests itself as the active qualities of hot, cold, wet and dry, and the passive qualities of fire, water, air and earth. These relate to the four primary colours: fire is red, hot and dry, air is yellow, hot and wet, earth is blue, cold and dry, and water is green, cold and wet.

Schemes of seven colours dominate the spiritual methods of some of the Sufi orders, each order adopting a different scheme. The Shaykh has the initiate concentrate on a colour, and what the initiate sees reveals the level attained. In the seven-colour

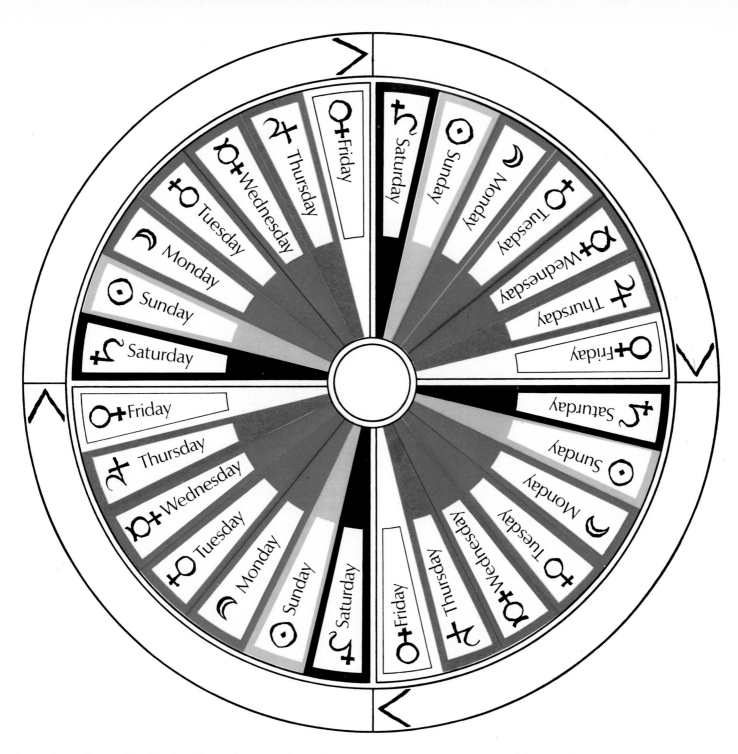

scheme shown here, white, black and sandalwood form a group of three complemented by the group of four: red, yellow, green and blue. The group of four relates to the qualities of Nature; the group of three relates to the qualities of the Spirit as It descends through light, expands horizontally upon the earth, and ascends through blackness.

In this colour scheme there is an alchemical marriage of Nature and Spirit. The scheme relates to the macrocosm, as each colour symbolizes a planet and a day of the week. It also relates to the microcosm, through the qualities of nature, hot, cold, wet and dry, and their transformation through motion into the Spirit. (Diagrams by Nader Ardalan and the author, from *The Sense of Unity.*)

دید و دریا و بر لب ساحل کرد شهزاده جهان منزل بو د آن روز تا بش سلطان

The complementarity of Divine Beauty and Majesty is often compared to the complementarity of the feminine and masculine principles, which are manifest in the universe and hidden in the mystic awaiting spiritual union. When the journey is described in terms of love, the highest form sought, the Beloved, is the feminine principle which is symbolized by the Divine Name of Beauty (*Jamāl*). Divine Beauty manifests expansion and displays the splendour of the world as a symbol of God. Divine Majesty (*Jalāl*) manifests contraction and reveals the limitations within things; the world is *only* a symbol of a higher Reality.

As the pair of Beloved and Lover, Divine Beauty and Majesty have been the subject of many love stories. All the Divine Names and Qualities are often described as aspects of one or the other; it is through the Names of Majesty that the world is created, and the mystic returns through the Names of Beauty. (Farrukhabakht seats Jalāl on the throne beside Jamāl; Jalāl, burning with love, reaches the sea of quicksilver; from ms. of *The Story of Jamāl and Jalāl*, 16th c.)

Psychological Symbols

The cypress tree symbolizes potential wholeness, for biologically it is a tree which contains the masculine and feminine principles within itself. It is a form which appears frequently in iconography. Known as the perfect Muslim because of its submission (*islām*) to the wind, it is in this wind-blown form that it is most often seen, as the paisley motif.

To the Sufis, the symbols found in woman are Divine realities; for she is the place of a Divine manifestation. The symbolism of woman is most often found in Sufi poetry, where a highly technical language of love was formed (see p. 21).

Whereas the eye, the niche of light, is directed outwards, the mouth draws one inwards. One eats and speaks by invoking one of the Names of God. Through invocation, in a sense, one consumes the Divinity and, by doing so, is oneself consumed.

The mole, the dot under the Arabic letter *bā*, symbolizes Divine Essence Itself, the Mystery, the abysmal darkness. It is single in itself but embraces all phenomena. With the Sufi, it corresponds to the Heart's centre; it is that to which desire is directed.

The mole symbolizes the Divine Essence in Its aspect of the Manifest, the Outward. The hair symbolizes the Divine Essence in Its aspect of the Hidden, the Inward; it is the symbol of multiplicity which hides unity. Multiplicity conceals the non-existence of things and thereby veils the Heart; but at the same time as the hair veils, it attracts Divine Grace and Divine Gifts. Like the face, the hair is veiled because of the sacred power it holds within itself. (*Qalamkār* cloth, Iran, 20th c.; A girl playing a drum, detail, by Abū'l Qāsim, Iran, 19th c.)

'The dancing is a reference to the circling of the spirit around the cycle of existing things on account of receiving the effects of the unveilings and revelations; and this is the state of the mystic. The whirling is a reference to the spirit's standing with God in its Secret [*sirr*] . . . the circling of its look and thought, and its penetrating the ranks of existing things. . . . And his leaping up is a reference to his being drawn from the human station to the station of union. . . .

'When they experience within them a stirring which affects them like the commotion of one who is called to the service of a mighty king and to appear before God,

he who falls into ecstasy does not rise till he is overpowered, and the people do as he does. . . . Then when their spirits receive a mystical apprehension of the unseen states, and their hearts are softened by the lights of the Divine Essence and are established in purity and the spiritual lights, they sit down, and he who chants, chants a light chant to bring them forth by degrees from the internal to the external.' (Aḥmad Ghazālī.)

(Muḥammad Tabadkani dancing in ecstasy, from ms. of *Majālis al-ʾUshshāg*, Turkey, 16th c.; darvishes dancing, Konya, Turkey, 20th c.)

Religious symbols

Religious symbols particular to Sufism begin with the place of retreat (see pp. 94–95), which in Persian is called a *khānaqāh*, in Turkish a *takyah* (the one shown here is the *takyah* of the Maulawī order in Konya) and in Arabic a *zawiyyah*. Its method of construction is always the same; the following relates to the building of an Algerian *zawiyyah*: 'The way in which this *zawiyyah* was built is both eloquent and typical. The architect was the Shaykh himself – not that he drew up a plan or manipulated a set-square. He simply said what he wanted, and his conception was understood by the builders. . . . Among the Shaykh's North African disciples there began an exodus in relays: masons came, carpenters, others, stone-cutters, workers on the roads, or even ordinary manual labourers. Here, in mid-twentieth century, was the same fervour that had built the cathedrals in the Middle Ages, and no doubt the actual building itself had taken place along somewhat the same lines.' (Marcel Carret, quoted by Martin Lings, *A Sufi Saint . . .*).

Sufi shrines serve as important religious symbols, for they relate to a higher level of Reality. Each shrine contains a symbolic significance to which the pilgrim relates. Shrines devoted to Khizr (Elijah, the Green Man) are most often visited by women who are not able to bear children. In the case of Haḍrat-i-Maʿsūmmah, sister of the eighth Shiʿite Imām Reẓa, because she died a young virgin, her shrine at Qom essentially draws pilgrims who relate to the concept of virginity. This concept recalls a sacred state, not only at the physical level, but at the psychic level as well. It is a state when the mystic's psyche is opened only to God. The concept of virginity is essential to one who 'brings forth' (p. 82) through a creative power that has been impregnated by the Spirit within. (*Takyah* of the Maulawī Order, Konya, Turkey; courtyard of the Shrine of Haḍrat-i-Maʿsūmmah, Qom, Iran, 16th c.)

The peacock has played an important role in Sufi poetry and iconography. 'As Light was manifested and saw Self reflected in a mirror for the first time,' a Sufi story relates, 'It saw Self as a peacock with its tail outspread.' The Light symbolizes the uniqueness of Divine Majesty. As it moves from contraction towards expansion It is transformed into the infinite richness of Divine Beauty, expansive and resplendent. The soul of the mystic is described in the same terms. When it reaches the Presence of Light, the Intellect, the soul moves from contraction to expansion, and comes to radiate from the centre in all directions in order to reflect upon all realities. These reflections which radiate out from the Eye of the Heart are as ornaments in the form of

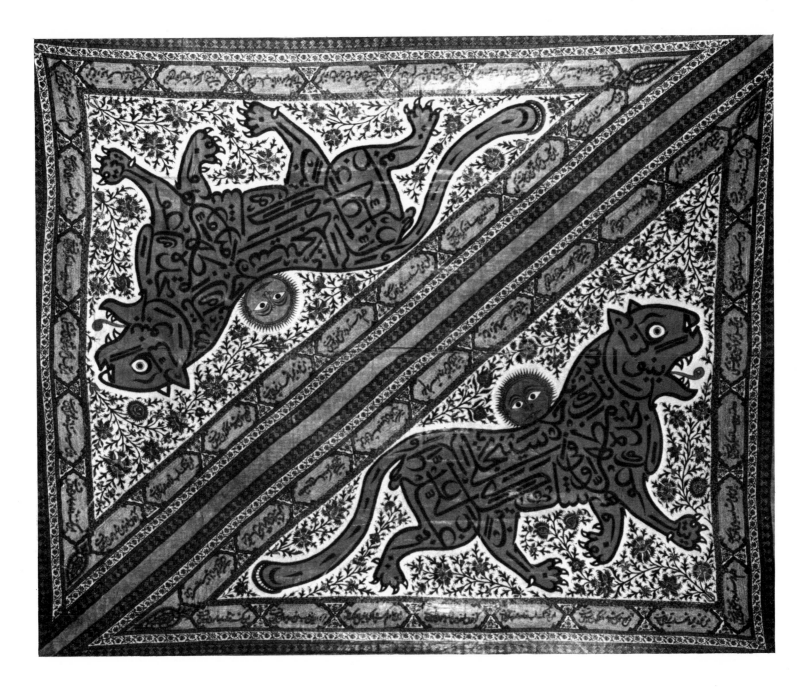

spiritual virtues which relate to the eyes in the tail of the peacock, brilliant centres of contraction in the midst of overall expansion.

The lion symbolizes action as opposed to contemplation; for it symbolizes gold and the sun, the active, directive, creative principle within all things. To some Sufis, the lion symbolizes the Universal Prototype, and also the Shaykh to whom the disciple owes everything received in the way of spiritual instruction and mystical experience. In Shiʿite circles, ʿAlī is often symbolized as the Lion of God; Jalāl al-Dīn Rūmī describes him as such in the *Mathnawī*. (*Qalamkār* cloths, Iran, 20th c.)

Gabriel, the Spirit, is not of the created world; those who do not know It are described as being veiled. They have been given only knowledge of the sensible world. To know the Gabriel within one's being is to have knowledge of God, the Most High; and 'those rooted in knowledge' (17 : 87) come to know this.

The wisdom of Abraham symbolizes the concept of the container and the contained. When food permeates into the body, the body contains it. The food hides itself in the form so that the form is apparent, but the food is hidden. When the Divinity is Transcendent, It is apparent and the creature is hidden, assimilated into all of the Names of God: into His hearing, His seeing, His attributes and His modes of knowledge. When an aspect of the Divine is Immanent, contained within the form, God is the hearing of the form, the sight, the hand and all the faculties.

Once Abraham had reached the degree of knowledge whereby he was called *Khalīl*, the intimate friend of God, he made hospitality a sacred rite. Nourishment penetrates the entire body until it is assimilated by its smallest parts. As the Divine has no parts, in the sense that the creature has, what is penetrated is the Divine Archetypes, the Names and Qualities of God through which the Divine manifests Itself. Human forms, and those other forms which humanity re-creates through symbolic ritual, are the place of Its manifestation: the receptacles for the Divinity. When one comes to know this, one reaches the station of Abraham, the intimate friend of God. (The Angel Gabriel showing the bravery of ʿAlī to the Prophet, detail from ms. of *Khawar Nameh*, by Ibn Haẓm, Shiraz, Iran, 1480; Abraham surrounded by flames, detail from ms. of *Anthology of Iskandar*, Shiraz, Iran, 1410.)

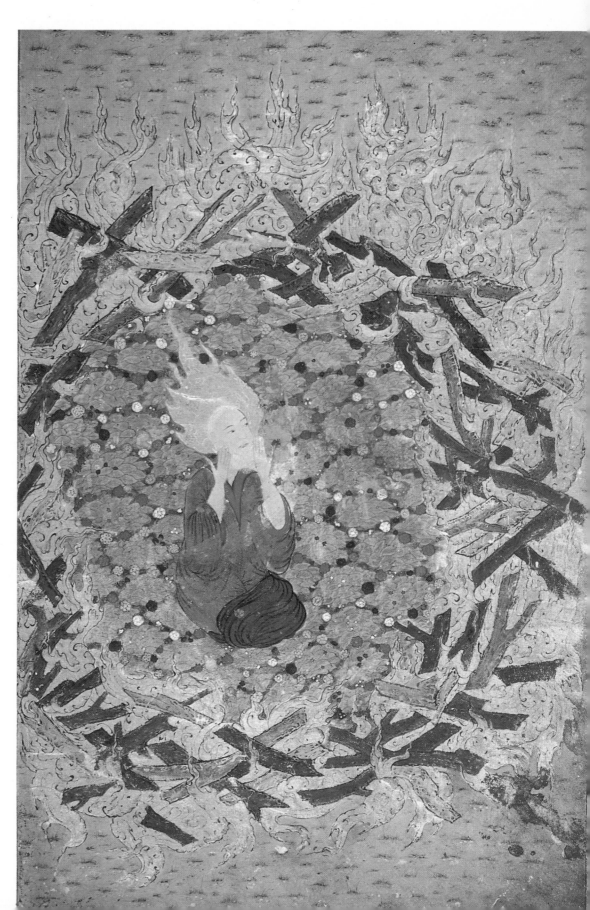

The room which serves as the place of retreat (khalwat) is sacred space to the Sufi. It is here that one invokes, silently or aloud, the Name of God.

The *iwān* or porch under which the Sufi meditates symbolizes the Way, or transitional space between the temporal and spiritual worlds. 'Metaphysically, the *iwān* can be viewed as the locus of the soul moving between the garden or court, taken as the Spirit, and the room, seen as the body. Its bisected form leaves it an incomplete form, capable only of uniting man to the Spirit and thereby accomplishing the *iwān*'s own reabsorption.' (Nader Ardalan.) (*Khāna-qāh*, mausoleum of Shaykh ʿAbd al-Samad al-Isfahānī, Natanz, Iran, 14th c.; *iwān*, Djomeh.)

Alexander, known in the Quran as Zul Qarnayn (18 : 82–93), the King with two horns, is seen here consulting the Seven Sages of antiquity, Thales, Anaxagoras, Anaximenes, Empedocles, Pythagoras, Socrates and Plato, before setting out on his spiritual journey. He is esoterically interpreted as the Heart of the mystic, which is King of the east and the west. The Heart's journey is beautifully described by Sufi interpreters of the Quran. The journey is through the way of physical attachments and awarenesses of the lower world until the Heart (Alexander, Zul Qarnayn) reaches the setting of the sun, the point of awakening. It sets in a muddy spring, the water of materiality. The Heart finds near this spring of darkness, the physical, sensory, psychic and spiritual faculties of the soul. The Heart subdues anger and lust by means of asceticism; at the same time, it strengthens its spiritual faculties of meditation and contemplation. Discernment within is awakened. Thereafter the Heart follows a second journey, the journey to God through spiritual purification and sanctification until it reaches the rising of the sun, the Spirit. It finds its spiritual faculties unveiled in the light. Then it follows the journey in God until it reaches a point between two barriers: its Divine nature and

كنيزان جلوه كرد در حجله ناز   همه دستان نما و عشوه پرداز

its original fallen nature. Here temptations increase until it builds its own wall out of knowledge and actions stemming from the Divine Law and spiritual practices. Only by building this wall is the Heart able to drive away the demonic psychic forces of Gog and Magog. It builds the wall of ingots of hot iron until the barriers and walls become one, level. It blows knowledge upon the iron, the actions or rites and rituals. Then it calls for molten copper of invocations and intentions to be poured over the walls. Thus it gains certitude. Psychic faculties can no longer scale the wall of the Divine Law, the rites of which have been strengthened by knowledge and sealed with invocation.

Just as Alexander is the symbol of Divine Wisdom, as expressed in mystical poetry through hymns of wisdom, so Joseph is the symbol of Divine Beauty, which so enraptures the soul that nothing of the self remains. Joseph is shown in the miniature with seven slave girls who each symbolize a stage of the soul in which each tries to use its charms to seduce him. (Alexander and the seven sages, from ms. of *Khamseh*, by Niẓāmī, Shiraz, Iran, 15th c.; Joseph enthroned, listening to music played by Zulaykha's maids, from ms. of *Yusuf u Zulaykha*, by Jamī, Tabriz, Iran, 1540.)

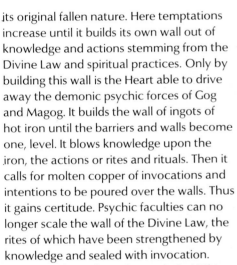

There are three important Divine Names relating to creation: *Khalq*, *Barī'* and *Muṣawwir*. *Khalq* is that aspect of creation which *conceives* of the possibilities of things, and is also known as the eternal wisdom or Sophia. This is the role the Virgin Mary symbolizes for the Sufi, as she was the receptive form which conceived the Spirit. *Barī'* is that aspect of the Creator which *brings forth*; the Virgin Mary further symbolizes this aspect of the Divine, in that she gave birth to the Word. The third name, *Muṣawwir*, is that aspect of the Creator which *embellishes* forms; it most often relates to craftsmen, artisans and architects who emulate the creative act of the Virgin Mary by conceiving and bringing forth the Spirit and nurturing it within sensible forms.

Fatima, the daughter of the Prophet, is called the Creative Feminine by the Sufis: 'It is the concept of the Creative Feminine which holds the secret of Lordship [the words of the Prophet, "one who knows self, knows Lord", see p.17]. The secret is to hold the nourishment of God with the substance of one's being and by one's being, give substance to the Divine Name one symbolizes' (H' Corbin, *Creative Imagination . . .*). Fatima symbolizes the essence of the feminine because she was the creator of the being (Logos) by whom she herself was created (i.e. Muḥammad ﷺ). That is, whereas the Virgin Mary is the mother of the Logos, Word, Fatima is the daughter of the Logos, who in turn, through her marriage to 'Alī, gave birth to the Logos as manifested in the Imāms. (The Nativity, from ms. of *Qiṣaṣ al-Anbiyā*, 16th c.; Fatima sitting by A'isha and Umm-Salma, from ms. Life of Muḥammad ﷺ, Turkey, 16th c.)

THE JOURNEY THROUGH GOD

Symbols of Transformation

Through symbols, one moves closer to transformation, the goal of the Quest. One of the most profound expressions of transformation is found in the Quranic verse: 'He is the First, and the Last, the Manifest and the Hidden, and He knows infinitely all things' (57 : 3).

The First is the origin of all things. It is the birth, the beginning, the centre and the point. The First is the knowledge of man in his primordial state; this is symbolized in Adam. The Adam of one's being relates to the world of nature and one's physical mould. His relation to the Prophet of Islam as the Universal Logos is expressed in the Prophet's words, 'I was conceived when Adam was between water and clay. Whoever hath seen me, hath seen the Truth.' Essentially, this tradition refers to the notion that a thought is completed before it is actualized.

It is at the centre, from which the First began, that the Last is found. The Last is death and reintegration with the Divine. The Last is the One to whom all return, and it is here that the Sufi fulfils the Tradition of the Prophet, 'Die before you die', in order to be reborn in the Hidden, the Self. The path to the Hidden begins at the centre, manifested in man by the inner intellect which is veiled by the ego. It is only by rending this veil that the mystic will be able to find Self, known only through discernment, invocation and contemplative meditation.

The Last is a temporal externalization: it is death and reintegration with the Divine. It is symbolized by the Prophet, whose nocturnal journey the Sufi emulates. The Prophet's bodily ascent to heaven occurred because of the Divine Grace which permeated his being. The ascent of the Sufi occurs on what is known as the Night of Power, when the heavens open and the Angels and Spirits descend. The Heart of the mystic is as the full moon; his soul is as the darkness of night. The Heart, now full, totally reflects the sun, which brings peace, tranquillity, until the break of dawn. The break of dawn is the moment when the peace is annihilated in the Light of the Absolute, leaving only the Absolute Peace of Unity. (Adam and Eve, from ms. of *Manafi al-Hayawān*, Maragha, Iran, 1294–99; The Ascent of the Prophet, from ms. of *Khamseh*, by Niẓāmī, Shiraz, Iran, 1410.)

The *chahār ṭāq* is an architectural symbol
of transformation. A mandala in plan; its
shape is that of a dome resting on a square.
Within this space, which resolves the transformation of the circle into the square, are
placed the *miḥrab* of a mosque, a font, and
a shrine to a saint. This space then symbolizes the Sufi's place of life, death and
spiritual rebirth.

The mandala, as a reflection of the cosmos and cosmic processes within all things, works through numbers and geometry, beginning with Unity, moving through Its theophany and back to Unity. It recapitulates at one and the same time, the permanence of Paradise as an idea and its impermanence as a temporal reality. To the mystic, it evokes the surrender to Self and the reintegration of the many into the One. (*Chahār tāq*, near Kashan, Iran, 19th c.; centre of the Ardabil carpet, Tabriz, Iran, *c.* 1540.)

The mystic has given birth to light, knowledge, his own Spirit, his perfect nature, in the dragon of the sky (p. 45), the cosmic womb where the eclipses of the sun and moon occur. Sitting upon fire, consumed by light and knowledge, the soul of the mystic is transformed into the full moon which then, as the station cools and contracts, becomes a crescent, the symbol of receptivity for the receiving of Divine Grace.

The mystic is attended to by Harut and Marut, two fallen angels who taught man the arts of magic. Four angels hold up the Throne upon which the mystic sits. According to Shah Ni'matullāh Wali, the four angels Gabriel, Michael, Seraphial and Azrail correspond to four aspects of the Name Allāh. The four letters A L L H correspond to the mystic's Heart, Intellect, Spirit and Soul, which have journeyed and united.

The symbol of the cobweb has many interpretations, but at the level of transformation it has been interpreted as the saying of the Sufis: 'I am but a message from God to God.' The web is as the message, woven from what is transformed within. The extent of the message is not important, just as the strength of the web is not in its size. Some Sufis left only one or two lines of thought; others, such as Ibn 'Arabī, left volumes of intuitive realizations. Whether one is guided by natural processes (in takwīnī) or by revealed tradition (in tashrī'ī), it is only through spiritual transformation at the centre that the Sufi saying is fulfilled. (Cobweb; mandala, from ms. of Kitāb al-diriyak, Mosul, Iraq, 1199.)

Darkness and light are the archetypical symbols of Sufism because they are natural, immediate self-expressions of a root experience of the Divinity. They denote the stations of annihilation (*fanā'*) and subsistence (*baqā'*). These stations are metaphysical experiences which occur only at a transcendental level of awareness.

In the station of *fanā'*, there is complete lack of consciousness of object or ego; one is moving towards darkness. There is not even any consciousness of the experience itself. There are no images.

In the station of *baqā'* the mind reawakens to the phenomenal world, but now these forms and images are objective forms in which the Divine Essence manifests Itself. In darkness, one is moving towards light.

Light and darkness are, for the Sufi, metaphorical experiences. Existence is light. When the Absolute appears to the consciousness of the mystic, It appears as uncontaminated unity, as light. All multiplicity disappears into darkness. Thus, when light makes its full appearance, all things disappear. Light causes darkness. But because all things lose their individuality and become obliterated from consciousness, the whole world paradoxically turns into an ocean of light. Out of the depths of this light all things that disappeared into darkness begin to be reborn in their individualities; but at this stage they are darknesses that are fully saturated with the Pure Light of existence. (Plaster window, Marrakesh, Morocco, 16th c.; stone grille, Friday Mosque, Isfahān, Iran, 12th c.)

Part 3
The 'How' of Mystical Expression

Subsistence (*baqā'*) is to know that the Beloved is devoted to the lovers upon whom Its belovedness depends. In this way, every lover is a beloved and every beloved is a lover. Love needs and desires beauty, and beauty needs and desires love. The Absolute, which is Absolute Beauty and Love, loves those who love It; and since it loves them, It leaves nothing of themselves in them; they are one with It for, in reality, It is the only beloved and the only lover.

In a Sacred Tradition attributed to 'Alī, the Divine says:

Who seeketh Me findeth Me
Who findeth Me knoweth Me
Who knoweth Me loveth Me
Who loveth Me, I love
Whom I love, I slay
Whom I slay, I must requite
Whom I must requite, Myself am the
* Requital*

(Khānaqāh ceiling, Māhān, Iran, 15th c.)

SPIRITUAL RETREAT
Khalwat

The retreat to an isolated cell in order to 're-member' God is considered by many orders to be the most important of all Sufi disciplines. It is an aid in achieving a state of permanent inward retreat. Observing the Traditions of the Prophet, who used to retreat to caves in the mountains, some orders still recommend one to retreat to the solitudes of nature. Other orders have isolated cells for the practice of the *khalwat*. Shaykh Al-'Alawī has described the *khalwat* as 'a cell in which I put the novice after he has sworn to me not to leave it for forty days if need be. In this oratory he must do nothing but repeat cease-lessly, day and night, the Divine Name (*Allāh*), drawing out with each invocation the syllable *ah* until he has no breath left. Previously he must have recited the *Shahādah* (*lā ilāha illa'Llah,* there is no god but God) seventy-five thousand times. During the [*khalwat*] he fasts strictly by day, breaking his fast only between sunset and dawn . . . Some *fuqarā* [mystics] obtain the sudden illumination after a few minutes, some only after several days, and some only after several weeks.' (Quoted by Martin Lings.)

The spiritual retreat can remain effective, after one leaves the *khalwat*, only if one continues to remember. To some, this remembrance is ex-pressed in arts and crafts. To others, the ex-pression of the Word Itself through constant in-vocation is their art. And yet others re-express the Word through poetry, music and other sciences.

The craftsmen who organize themselves in guilds (*aṣnāf*) or chivalric orders (*futuwwat*) are those who remember through artistic ex-pression. Every traditional master craftsman was an initiate of a Sufi order – as some still are today. The master's success in continuing to in-voke through his work determines the spiritual strength of the entire guild, as expressed in its work. The other members of the guild imple-ment the designs, and while they may not be fully conscious of all the principles involved, their creative expressions attest to their Spirit, which will lie dormant within until their own *khalwat* awakens it.

The *futuwwat* (or *fedeli d'amore* as they are called in allusion to Dante) have nine grades in their orders. The first three are those of all trade guilds: apprentice, journeyman and master. The second three relate to ceremonies, and the last three are the Shaykh and his representatives. Members are those who are committed either by their words or by partaking of the ritual cup of salt water.

Many of the concepts of the *futuwwat* were expressed in mystical prose and poetry. Like the institutions of knighthood and chivalry, this tradition travelled all over the Islamic lands; it is still very much alive today.

The *fedeli d amore* place a special emphasis upon the Prophet Solomon, as he symbolizes the Wisdom of Compassion, which is their creed. The Queen of Sheba, Bilqīs, is their feminine ideal, like Dante's Beatrice; she is the Eternal Sophia manifested in the aspect of Beauty. Bilqīs is the form through which one contemplates a radiant source of light which is theophanic Beauty. She is contemplated as Essence no longer veiled by the Names and Qualities; for it is through her that the Face of God is manifested. She is the Eternal Feminine which is hidden within the self.

Within all the Sufi orders, including both *aṣnāf* and *futuwwat*, a division arises between those who are in a station of intoxication (*sukr*) and those in a station of sobriety (*ṣaḥw*). Those seekers known as intoxicates are usually followers of the great Persian Saint Abū Yazīd Basṭāmī. The founder of the 'ecstatic' school of Sufism, he is famous for the boldness of his expression of the mystic's complete absorption in the Godhead. This station (which can come upon the mystic as a transient state; see pp. 98–99) is characterized by loss of sanity and self-control. The soul becomes intoxicated, expansive with the wine of Knowledge of the Divine, enraptured by the contemplation of God.

The second group are the mystics known for their sobriety. According to this group, which has a larger following than the previous one, intoxication is only the beginning of oneness. Perfect oneness is attained in sobriety, when the self, having been restored to consciousness, knows itself to be but a mirror in which the Divine Essence reflects upon Itself.

The relationship between the two stations has been expressed by Ibn Fārīd in the following way: 'Existence is a veil in the beginning of the mystic life, and also in its middle stage, but not in its end. The mystic is veiled in the beginning by the outward aspect of existence [created things] from the inward aspect [God], while in the middle stage [period of intoxication during which the mystic has no consciousness of phenomena] he is veiled by its inward aspect [God] from its outward aspect [created things]. But when he has reached his goal [sobriety], neither do created things veil him from God nor does God veil him from created things, but God reveals Himself to the mystic in both His aspects at once [as the Creator and as the universe of created things], so that he sees with his bodily eye the beauty of the Divine Essence manifested under the attribute of the Outward.' (R. Nicholson.)

This transformation most often begins under the direction of a Shaykh, a living spiritual guide, in the *khalwat*, the spiritual retreat devoted to the remembrance of God and the forgetting of self.

From far left:

Shrines such as this, from the bazaar of Kāshān, Iran, act as gateways for people whose everyday lives bring them past this place. Some are awakened to further possibilities of the Way; some are content with this form alone.

The room of prayer of the Maulawī order at Konya, Turkey.

An example of a remote shrine in Iran. This serves the villagers and nomadic tribesmen who rarely venture to the city.

A Sufi who could be described as being in the station of intoxication.

A Sufi master calligrapher of the Qaderi order who could be described as being in the station of sobriety.

A rug showing a Sufi Master, Nūr 'Alī Shāh.

X SUPREME GOAL

100	unity	3:16
99	gathering	8:17
98	solitude	24:25
97	subtraction	20:12
96	discovery	4:110
95	concealment	6:9
94	realization	2:262
93	subsistence	20:75
92	annihilation	55:26
91	gnosis	5:86

VIII SANCTITY

80	stability	30:60
79	absence	12:84
78	drowned	37:103
77	exile	11:118
76	breath	7:140
75	the secret	11:33
74	joy	10:59
73	purity	38:47
72	a moment	20:42
71	secret glance	7:139

IX REALITIES

90	separation	3:27
89	union	53:9
88	sobriety	34:22
87	intoxication	7:139
86	expansion	42:9
85	contraction	25:48
84	life	6:122
83	beholding	25:47
82	contemplation	50:36
81	unveiling	53:10

V PRINCIPLES

50	without desires	28:86
49	spiritual richness	93:8
48	poverty	35:16
47	invocation	18:23
46	intimacy	2:182
45	certainty	51:20
44	discipline	9:113
43	will	17:86
42	resolution	3:154
41	purpose	4:101

VI VALLEYS

60	spiritual power	53:17
59	peacefulness	89:27
58	tranquillity	48:4
57	inspiration	27:40
56	reverence	71:12
55	sagacity	15:75
54	spiritual sight	12:108
53	wisdom	2:272
52	knowledge	18:64
51	goodness	55:60

VII MYSTICAL STATES

70	spiritual taste	38:49
69	flashes	20:9
68	distraction	7:140
67	bewilderment	12:31
66	ecstasy	18:13
65	thirst	6:76
64	anxiety	20:86
63	nostalgia	29:4
62	jealousy	38:32
61	love	5:59

I GATEWAY

10	audition	8:23
9	ascetism	23:60
8	fleeing	51:50
7	hold fast	22:78
6	meditation	40:13
5	reflection	16:44
4	conversion	39:54
3	reckon with	59:18
2	repentance	49:11
1	awakening	34:45

II DOORS

20	yearning	21:90
19	hope	33:21
18	devotion	73:8
17	scruples	74:4
16	self denial	11:86
15	enjoying quiet	22:35
14	humility	57:15
13	concern	52:26
12	fear	16:52
11	sorrow	9:92

III CONDUCT

30	full submission	4:68
29	reliance	28:6
28	commitment	40:47
27	trust	5:26
26	rectitude	41:5
25	amending	6:76
24	sincerity	39:3
23	respect	22:30
22	fix attention	9:10
21	vigilance	57:27

IV CHARACTER

40	largesse	7:154
39	generosity	18:12
38	modesty	25:64
37	firmness	68:4
36	preference	59:9
35	being true	47:23
34	bashfulness	96:14
33	grateful	34:12
32	satisfied	89:27
31	patience	16:128

STAGES OF THE JOURNEY

When one is at the *gateway*, the beginning of the journey to the Absolute, there are various states which descend upon the mystic. Each one is itself a gateway orienting the seeker to the journey ahead. Anṣārī has described the stages or houses as being ten tens.

This of necessity leads to the *doors* which must be entered. These are the second stage of the journey. The minute one enters the door, one comes in need of actions, encounters; one meets these with *conduct* which relates to the states one feels and to this, the third stage.

After encountering one's more perfect self, one learns good habits and dispositions from others and thus builds *character* by creating praiseworthy forms of self; this is the fourth stage.

From this stage one is readied for the best forms of purity, and a goodness of character has been created which is really the fruit of one's conduct. At this stage, it is necessary that *principles* be followed, which become the foundation of one's life; this is the fifth stage.

In the motion of acting and seeking the Way, one comes upon precipices; and difficulties will occur in the stage of the *valleys*. After this, the sixth stage, one reaches the level of the various accidental spiritual *states*; this is the seventh stage.

The eighth stage, known as *sanctity*, is the stage where spiritual powers make their appearance. This is the gathering after separation, where one is dominated by good human qualities and they are acquired.

In the next stage, *realities*, one becomes negligent in oneself and is immersed in one's Lord and the Divine Self, where one's actions are all directed towards the Absolute. This is the ninth stage of the journey. The tenth stage is the stage of subsistence in God, the *supreme goal*, the stage of union.

The stages are described in other terms by Simnānī, who relates the macrocosmic Descent of creation to the microcosmic Ascent of the return. From the Divine Essence to the world of nature-man, there are seven levels, from light to shadow. On the return, one passes these seven stages in reverse order, ascending through seven subtle, non-physical aspects of self.

These seven subtle stages relate to the seven major Prophets of Semitic monotheism. When one reaches the Truth of one's being, one has

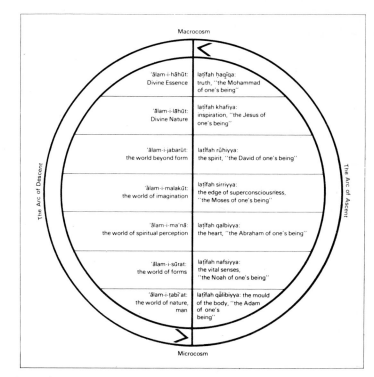

become the Universal Prototype, having been transformed into the Muḥammad of one's being.

These seven Prophets and seven stages correspond to seven colours, described variously by the various orders.

To Simnānī, the Adam of one's being is the acquiring of an embryonic mould of a new body, a subtle, non-physical form. The psychological colour of this stage is black moving towards dark grey.

The second organ newly activated corresponds to the animal soul, the battlefield of vital and organic operations, which is the centre of desires and evil passions. This corresponds to the Noah of one's being, because Noah faced the same situation in dealing with the hostility of his people. The colour of this stage is blue.

The third subtle organ is the spiritual Heart, which exists in an embryonic form in the potential mystic as the pearl within a shell. It is none other than the True I, the personal individuality. The spiritual I relates to the Abraham of one's being, as Abraham was the intimate friend of God. This stage is red. The Abraham of one's being travels the subtle centres of supraconsciousness.

The fourth subtle organ is the Secret (see p. 8), the point of supraconsciousness, and is the stage of spiritual monologues which correspond to those in which Moses participated. The colour is white.

The fifth subtle organ is the Spirit, which because of the nobility of its rank is invested as the vice-regent of God, the David of one's being. Its colour is yellow.

The sixth subtle organ is that which receives inspiration. It is the Jesus of one's being, because it is this organ which announces the Name. The colour of this stage is luminous black.

The seventh subtle organ which is activated is the Muḥammad of one's being, which corresponds to one's Divine centre or Eternal Seal, as Muḥammad was the Seal of Prophecy. The colour of this stage is green.

Left and above:

Chart of the Virtues which correspond to the ten stages of the Journey according to ʿAbd Allāh Anṣārī al-Harawī, with the Quranic references from which their names are drawn. See Anṣārī, *Les Etapes des itinérants vers Dieu.*

The stages of ascent and descent according to ʿAlāʾ al-dawlah Simnānī. Chart from Ardalan and Bakhtiar, *The Sense of Unity*, with corrections.

SPIRITUAL STATES: *Ahwāl*

Describing the journey in its *stages* (pp. 96–97) is the most removed form of description; it reflects only rational understanding. The means of psychological participation are referred to as *states*, *stations* and *presences*.

The word state (*ḥāl*) means 'to descend, alight or penetrate a place'; it denotes a quality which is not permanent. According to the Sufis, whatever change enters the heart by means of pure love from the direction of the Truth, without the deliberation or intention of the seeker, is called a spiritual state (*ḥāl*). It enters the mystic's heart through desire, anxiety, thirsting, bewilderment, illumination or intuition. It may occur as a flash, or it may remain longer, but it is never permanent. Feelings or emotions change or vanish, and the subject finally becomes weary.

That which descends is like music. Musical tones are part of the external world and natural phenomena; they are produced by vibrations; but they are expressed only when there is an encounter, when someone hears them or feels

them. Similarly, in spiritual states, a form receives and is thereby activated.

'To put it metaphorically: the ground in which tones fall is itself in wave motion. The wave is the metre; rhythm arises from the different arrangements of tones on the wave. . . . The tones may be distributed over the measure regularly or irregularly; may fill the measure in rapid succession or leave it empty for long stretches; at one place crowd close together, at another spread thin. . . . This freedom of distribution and arrangement makes it possible for the tones to give the constant basic form of the wave a changing, perpetually different profile. . . . This playing with the wave by the tones, this shaping of the substance of the wave; the conjunction and opposition of two components, their mutual tension and continuous adjustment to each other – this, in music, we experience as rhythm.' (V. Zuckerkandl.) The repetition of the tones is twofold: it satisfies the demand of symmetry to be completed, and it acts as a link in a chain of intensification.

Spiritual states and musical tones, which are mutable, impermanent qualities requiring an encounter or place in which to descend and then change the rhythm, both find a visual correspondence in the arabesque.

The arabesque is a form which harmoniously renders a constantly changing rhythmical motion. Varying in density over the surface, it is a rhythmic outpouring of thought given precision by parallels, inversions and interlacings.

Through rhythm and change, spiritual states are mutable conditions in which one is ignorant of the end and cannot predict the beginning. The mystic, much like the arabesque, is obliged to remain within the boundaries which the object of service demands. Spiritual states are instantaneous successions and alterations reflecting a transient spiritual mood. Their arrival and disappearance depend solely upon God. The arabesque, as it expresses the profusion of rhythms throughout the Universe, corresponds to the Divine gifts which one may receive but can never earn.

Ḥāl/waqt. These three figures are from Pope and Ackerman.

Ḥāl/tamkīn.

Talwīn/tamkīn.

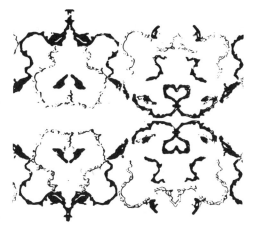

Spiritual State and Moment of Encounter: Ḥāl/Waqt

A spiritual state (ḥāl) is expressed as being both complementary to the moment of encounter (waqt) and the opposite of stability (tamkīn). The spiritual state evokes the impact of an encounter with a moment of time. The moment itself is the unit of psychic measurement of the encounter. It is the moment of time which allows the spiritual state to descend upon it and adorn it. The actualization of a spiritual state makes it possible not to lose the moment, and it is because of the moment of the encounter that the spiritual state is actualized in the soul. The moment is as the centre of an arabesque, actualizing the spirals, as the spirals, through their very existence, actualize the centre.

Spiritual State and Stability: Ḥāl/Tamkīn

A spiritual state refers to a multiplicity of emotions in the soul. These emotions reflect both discontinuity in their order and difficulty in their stabilization. The transient spiritual state, the internal reality of a self which is unstable to begin with, becomes stabilized as it moves towards tamkin: strengthening, stability, symmetry. The weak soul cannot persist in the act of a spiritual state which may arise, vanish, give way to some new favour. The mystic, endowed with repose, steadfastness and stability, becomes stabilized beyond the reach of every psychological change. This is readily expressed in the arabesque, where the rhythmic forms of the spirals of spiritual states are stabilized through symmetry.

Change and Stability: Talwīn/Tamkīn

Talwīn indicates change, an alternating transition from one state to another, whereas tamkīn is the act of enduring, stability, symmetry. 'The beginning of love is search,' the Sufi says, 'but the end is rest.' Stability and symmetry is the removal of the vacillation of change.

It is in strengthening (tamkīn), expressed as stability and symmetry, that one finds spiritual stations as distinct from states.

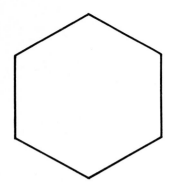 + 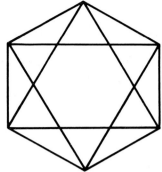 =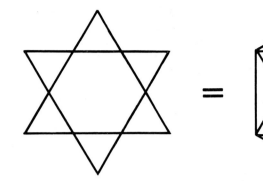

SPIRITUAL STATIONS
Maqāmāt

Spiritual stations are degrees of ascent, reached through certain rites and certain difficulties. They are permanent acquisitions, as opposed to states, which are gratuitous gifts that come and go with the attraction of the Divine. States, like the arabesque, express rhythm and continual change; the stations have places of staying and a respect for centre, and correspond in visual terms to geometric forms.

Geometric forms indirectly contain a duality which can be described through static and dynamic geometry (see chart on p. 105). Static geometry is the geometry of lines, whereas dynamic forms are expressions of points. Each descent from the Divine Essence is a nuptial union, a conjunction of two opposites, active and passive, with a view to a production of a third. The union of active and passive, the masculine and feminine principles within things, is repeated at every plane of being.

The polarization which is expressed in geometry through static and dynamic forms corresponds exactly to the inseparable pairs of complementary spiritual stations between which the seeker constantly moves:
contraction/expansion (*qabḍ/bast*);
gathering/separation (*jamʿ/tafriqah*);
sobriety/intoxication (*ṣaḥw/sukr*);
annihilation/subsistence (*fanāʾ/baqāʾ*);
presence/absence (*shuhūd/ghabat*).

Now, as the passive and active aspects unite in geometric form to create a third form and from there generate new forms, so too the mystic through spiritual practices acquires a stability, a symmetry of form which then generates new

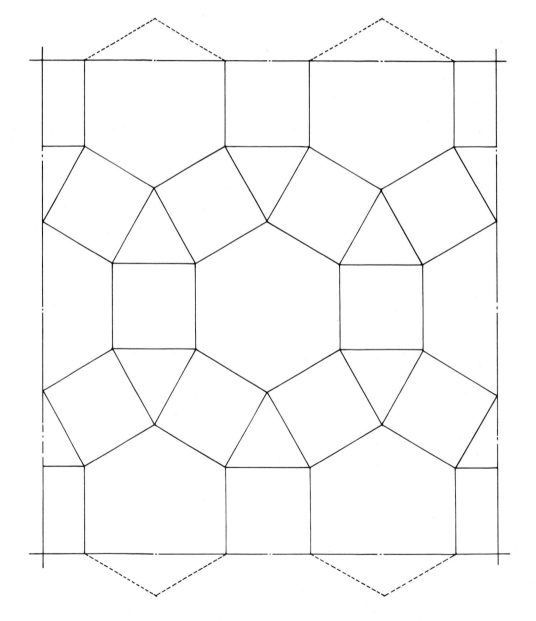

stations. But just as the geometric form never loses its successive generations (its connectedness moving with it), so the mystic, on achieving each new spiritual station, carries the knowledge of the previous stations with him.

Form dwells in its geometry; the Sufi dwells in the stations. Unlike arabesques, which play with a surface, geometric forms fill it to completion. So, too, the spiritual states as Divine gifts come and go, playing with the feelings of the mystic's form, whereas stations fill it completely. It is only then that a further station can be reached.

Every station has its own science, and like geometric forms, has a beginning and an end, which relate to the laws of similitude and symmetry. In this each one is expressive of a personality of the number to which it relates, and which gives expression only in a closed form.

Just as geometry brings order and structure to the seeming chaos of nature, so too the spiritual stations act as organizing forms for the soul. If left only with spiritual states, without the possibility of permanence amidst change, the mystic would easily lose control.

From far left:

Passive form+active form=complete form.

Generation of form inward to the centre.

Generation of form outward from the centre.

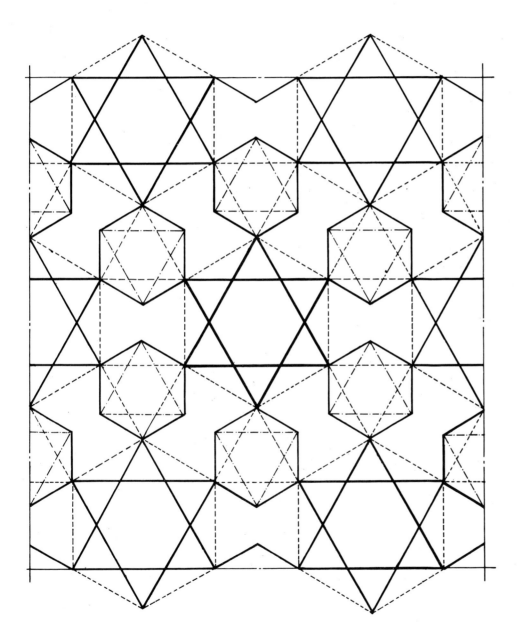

Gathering and Separation: Jam'/Tafriqah

The mystic who achieves the station of gathering (*jam'*) has repelled the material world of phenomena, whereas the mystic who acquires the station of separation (*tafriqah*) is confirming devotion and God, while attached to the phenomenal world and separating the Absolute from Its creation. One who 'sees the world dark' is in the state of separation, regarding self as an individual and part. This is the view of multiplicity, which is the usual view of the phenomenal world.

Whereas the station of gathering is to 'behold one moon plainly', to be conscious of nothing but Unity, the highest station of gathering is the 'gathering of the gathering' (*jam' al-jam'*), where one 'beholds three moons together': that is to see Divine Unity in three aspects at one and the same time: Essence, Creator, Creatures; or Essence, Qualities, Actions; or Law, Way, Truth.

But just as there can be no masculine principle without a feminine one, no active without a corresponding hidden or apparent passive, the stations are fulfilled only through their opposites. Gathering without separation is known as impiousness; separation without gathering is uselessness. Together they form a conjunction of opposites: they join souls (place of gathering) with forms (separate realities). When these are joined, one has the unity of existence. The mystic is joined to the Spirit in the station of gathering, and to the body in the station of separation. Whosoever in devotion and prayers remembers self is in separation. Whosoever remembers God's grace is in gathering. Whosoever sees neither self nor deeds is in the gathering of the gathering. Gathering conceals and veils objects; separation conceals and veils God in Creation.

Presence and Absence: Shuhūd/Ghabat

To be present is to witness consciously; to be absent corresponds to unconscious, not actualized, witnessing. To be present, which corresponds to conscious remembrance, is to be as a mirror, reflective, aware in witnessing: it is to be aware of the Divine Presence, as the Tradition states: 'to worship God as if you saw Him, and if you do not see Him, He sees you'.

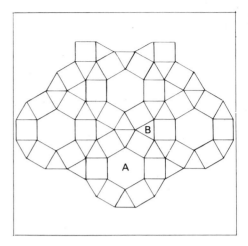

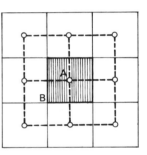

Jam', gathering (A), and *tafriqah*, separation (B), in a tile pattern at the Imamzadah 'Abd Allāh Ansārī, Gāzar Gāh, Iran.

Shuhūd, presence (A), and *ghabat*, absence (B), in a brickwork pattern at the Masjid-i-Ḥakīm, Isfahān, Iran.

PRESENCES : *Hadrat*

Calligraphic skill lies not only in the mastery of the individual forms but also in their relationships to the surrounding space: the balance and rhythm of form and non-form. Calligraphy, when it adopts the forms of the arabesque, deals with time and the infinite rhythms created by the encounter of objects with space within defined borders. This form of calligraphy speaks to the mystic states; the Word descends as a gratuitous gift of the Divine, setting up change and rhythm within the mystic's soul.

Calligraphy also encompasses the full expressive range of geometrical form, evoking a timeless quality that allows it to be integrated into every sort of surface adornment. As the Word in sensible form, its presence breathes life into compositions and emphasizes particular concepts through Quranic allusions. In architecture, through its placing between the dome and its square base, it enhances the symbolic transformation through its own transcendent forms.

As the Word descends through the Name of Compassion (*Rahmān*) upon all forms indiscriminately, so the Word is expressed in rhythmic arabesques; as the Word is the means whereby one ascends through the Name of Mercy (*Rahīm*), which rewards only acts performed, so it is expressed in geometric, structured, symmetrical forms.

'God establishes His Names and then effaces them in Presence' so a Tradition relates. Divine Presences are states or stations in which the Absolute reveals Itself to the mystic in one of the forms of the Divine Names. God is present in His Name at the same moment as He is absent: this doctrine of immanence and transcendence is never to be forgotten by the Sufi

Calligraphy, the most sacred of art forms, recalls the Word by which God calls Himself. In architecture this is most often found on the band between the base of a mosque and its dome.

This transitional space is the way of the return through the Word of God, the Quran as revealed to Muḥammad (ﷺ).

Calligraphy is thus the visual body of the Divine revelation, sacred in both form and content. Corresponding to the iconographic image of Christ in Christianity, the calligraphic form symbolizes the Word Itself, and its very presence obviates the use of any imagery.

The structure of calligraphy, composed of horizontal and vertical strokes woven into a rich fabric, is potent with symbolism. The verticals, like the warp of a carpet, provide an ontological relationship and a structure for the design, while the horizontals, like the weft, correspond to the creation that develops the balance and flow of the basic conception. It is through the harmonious weaving of the horizontal and the vertical that unity is achieved. The vertical and horizontal weavings correspond to the active and passive qualities contained in all things, and, just as calligraphy is woven together into a conjunction of horizontal and vertical, so too the mystic in his spiritual mode, through continual, uninterrupted repetition of invocation, unites his own inner complementary opposites.

Arabesque calligraphy. These four figures are from Ardalan and Bakhtiar, *The Sense of Unity.*

Arabesque calligraphy.

Geometric calligraphy.

Geometric calligraphy.

103

NUMBERS AND GEOMETRY
ʿIlm-i-aʿdād, Hindisah

To this point, we have followed the mystic through the encounters which descend, or to which the mystic ascends, upon the Way. The stages of the journey are, in a sense, a descriptive geography which serves to orient the mystic. Spiritual states and stations and presences are, further, detailed orientations expressed through art forms. There are, however, further levels of realization to be explored through the sciences themselves that Sufis, who are not necessarily practising craftsmen, have explored after their leaving the khalwat.

The first two sciences to be explored are very close to the architectural art forms we have just witnessed. Known as the sciences of numbers and geometry (ʿilm-i-aʿdād, hindisah), the principles involved formed a basis for many further sciences.

Some Sufi groups consider numbers as the principles of being and the root of all sciences; they express them as the first effusion of the Spirit or Intellect upon the soul. 'Number is the spiritual image resulting in the human soul from the repetition of Unity,' write the Ikhwān al-Ṣafāʿ, the Brethren of Purity. The Universe begins with One, descends through the multiple states of Being, and ends with the place of the gathering, the human form.

It is through geometry that the personality and character of numbers is revealed, providing still another means of coming to know the cosmic processes of nature. The number 1 generates the point, 2 the line and 3 the triangle. The triangle is the first form to enclose space in the generation of points or lines from 1. It symbolizes the action of the Intellect (2) on the Soul (3) and thereby brings about the descending, horizontal or ascending motion of the Intellect (see p. 50). Because the Intellect (as the active, masculine element) and the Soul (as the receptive, feminine element) represent a duality of manifestation from the One, their union and product, matter, forms the stability of the universe.

This same relationship is found in the science of spiritual alchemy. It is expressed in a medieval text in the following way: 'Know that the goal of the science of the Ancients is that from which all things proceed – the invisible and immobile God, whose Will brings into being the Intelligence. From out of the Will and the Intelligence appears the Soul in its unity; from the soul are born the distinct natures, which in turn generate the composed bodies. Thus one sees that a thing can be known only if one knows what is superior to it. The soul is superior to Nature, and it is by it that Nature can be known. The intelligence is superior to the soul, and it is by it that the soul can be known. Finally, the intelligence cannot but lead back to that which is superior – that is, to the One God who envelops it and whose Essence is imperceptible.' S. H. Nasr, Science and Civilization in Islam).

The creation of shapes through the use of numbers and geometry, as mathematical expressions, recalls the Archetypes reflected through the World of Symbols. Mathematics, then, is a language of the Intellect, a means of spiritual hermeneutics whereby one can move from the sensible to the intelligible world.

Table of numerical correspondences, from Ardalan and Bakhtiar, The Sense of Unity, based on the cosmology of the Ikhwān al-Ṣafāʿ, as described in S. H. Nasr, An Introduction to Islamic Cosmological Doctrines.

Number	Geometry Static	Geometry Dynamic	MACROCOSM		MICROCOSM		MATHEMATICAL ATTRIBUTES
0			Divine Essence		Divine Essence		
1			Creator	One Primordial Permanent Eternal	Creator	One Primordial Permanent Eternal	The point The principle and origin of all numbers
2			Intellect	Innate Acquired	Body divided into two parts	Left Right	One-half of all numbers are counted by it
3			Soul	Vegetative Animal Rational	Constitution of animals	Two extremities and a middle	Harmony First odd number One-third of all numbers are counted by it
4			Matter	Original Physical Universal Artifacts	Four humors	Phlegm Blood Yellow bile Black bile	Stability First square number
5			Nature	Ether Fire Air Water Earth	Five senses	Sight Hearing Touch Taste Smell	First circular number
6			Body	Above Below Front Back Right Left	Six powers of motion in six directions	Up, down, front, back, left, right	First complete number The number of surfaces of a cube
7			Universe	Seven visible planets and seven days of the week	Active powers	Attraction Sustenance Digestion Repulsion Nutrition Growth Formation	First perfect number
8			Qualities	Cold, dry Cold, wet Hot, wet Hot, dry	Qualities	Cold, dry Cold, wet Hot, wet Hot, dry	First cubic number and the number of musical notes
9			Beings of this world	Mineral Plant Animal (Each containing three parts)	Nine elements of the body	Bones, brain, nerves, veins, blood, flesh, skin, nails, hair	First odd square and last of single digits
10			The Holy Tetractys	First four universal Beings	Basic disposition of the body	Head, neck, chest, belly, abdomen, thoracic cavity, pelvic girdle, two thighs, two legs, two feet	Perfect number First of two-digit numbers
12			Zodiac Aries, Leo, Saggitarius Taurus, Virgo, Capricorn Gemini, Libra, Aquarius Cancer, Scorpio, Pisces	*Fire, hot, dry, east Earth, cold, dry, south Air, hot, wet, west Water, cold, wet, north*	Twelve orifices of the body	Two eyes, two nostrils, two ears, two nipples, one mouth, one navel, two channels of excretion	First excessive number
28			Stations of the Moon (divided into four quarters)	Each quarter equals one week, seven days represent seven planets	Twenty-eight vertebrae		Second complete number
360			Number of solar days		Number of veins in the body		Number of degrees in a circle

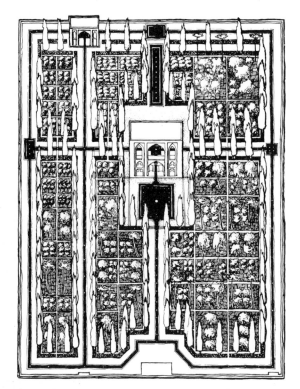

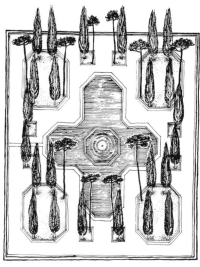

Generic Forms

It is through geometry and numbers that the generation of architectonic forms occurs. The architect is known as *muhandis*, the geometer. Music was as important as geometry in the traditional education system, and thus the geometer-to-be was steeped in both spatial and temporal forms.

Traditional architectonic forms, like the *radīf* of Persian music, constitute the philosophy of expression and the repertoire of a Shaykh, passed on to his students. Both architecture and music relate to schools of thought where the master is he who knows the repertoire perfectly.

A *radīf* has no rhythm, for it is, in a sense, forms of expression kept in a passive state until activated by a musician; so, too, traditional forms of architecture. The laws of expression are based on interpretation and improvisation, but the form remains at an archetypal level to be called upon and activated by a master.

The generic forms that we first explore, the repertoire of traditional architecture, such as garden, courtyard, minaret, dome, *chahār tāq* (p. 85), gateway (p. 42), porch (p. 79) and socle, are coalesced into mosque, *madrasah*, caravanserai and *tīmchah* (see pp. 108–09). But it is the generic forms that we first explore: the *radīf* of traditional architecture.

Garden and Courtyard: Bāgh/Hayāt. The garden and the courtyard are important forms in the concept of Paradise. The garden is traditionally an enclosure planted with trees surrounding a central pavilion. The whole becomes a mandala (pp. 86–87), providing both a centrifugal movement, outward into the paradise of nature, and a centripetal movement, inward, through its four porches, to the water, its spiritual centre. Generating ever-expanding ripples, the fountain recommences the cycle of conscious expansion and contraction.

The idea of the courtyard paralleled that of the open garden plan. . . . The courtyard plan, which generates a centripetal force, is more feasible as an urban form, capable of providing that basic contact with nature so essential to Iranian life. This plan dominates the architectural ac-

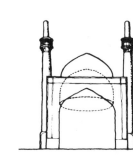

tivity of "place making" [makān], and within the Islamic period becomes the model of makān, unifying house with mosque, caravanserai with college, the individual parts with the whole. This unity is achieved through the visual interaction of space, shape and surface, complemented by their qualitative correspondences. Space, as the place of the "hidden treasure" of the house, is enclosed by shape, just as in man the body encloses the soul which encompasses the Spirit. Walls are thus a prerequisite for defining and isolating this sacred place within which the soul can be sensed and its spiritual quest fulfilled. The interaction of shape and surface must create a space that is totally at rest, devoid of tensions and conducive to contemplation. Such a solidified shape is to be found in the cube, a perfect form whose symbolic essence is stability, man, and the earthly paradise. Within this tranquil space, the placement of the traditional pool provides a centre as a positive direction for the creative imagination. Thus the horizontal creation of man is linked to the Vertical Cause, and man's recapitulation of paradise is complete.' (Ardalan and Bakhtiar, *The Sense of Unity*.)

Minaret and Dome: Minar/Gunbad. The minaret reflects the vertical and transcendent dimension of man's otherwise two-dimensional material existence. It represents man, who alone among the creatures stands upright; and it recalls the soul, aspiring to return to its origin.

The movement of the minaret from isolation towards the dome is a reintegration. Its pairing, to flank the portal and lead into the sanctuary, is a realization of the balance of creation, marking the axial approach to the ultimate unity of the dome.

Archetypically, the dome is the Divine Throne, passive to the Intellect, maternal and timeless. The Sufi concept of the centre, circle and sphere inherent in things is realized in the dome, seen as the Divine Spirit which encompasses the universe. The movement of this Spirit is viewed as either downward and expansive, *from* unity, or upward and contractive, *towards* the unity represented by the apex of the vault.

Spatial Connection Systems

The form of a traditional city is based on its movement systems, of which the most important architecturally is the order of the bazaar. Each system, like a mode or *dastgāh* in music, is the most stable and least changeable part of a given expressive form.

Essentially, the bazaar is the line which ties the city into a totality as it moves between two points, the entrance and exit to the city itself. As the musical mode gives scale and structure to the overall composition, so too the line of the bazaar gives the overall scale and structure of the city's form.

Each mode (*dastgāh*) of Persian music has its own special repertoire of melodies (*gūshah-hā*) which explore the most characteristic aspects of the mode. The melodies evolve from the mode in a system corresponding to the traditional spatial connection system.

The spatial connection system of the bazaar dictates how one moves between encounter points. While traversing the line of the bazaar you meet first the *dependent* indoor spaces. These spaces rely for their existence upon the primary, secondary or nodal spaces, such as stores and shops along the bazaar route. Occasionally you come upon another kind of opening, and this leads to *nodal* spaces. Nodal outdoor spaces, as seen in the caravanserai which stems from the primary movement system, are essentially rooms around a courtyard. Nodal indoor spaces, as seen in the *timchah,* are essentially rooms around a covered courtyard; there is usually a central pool, and the roof often has an open oculus. This encounter between dependent and nodal spaces and the primary movement system always unfolds in a ternary process of connection, transition and culmination. It is in this same way that a leaf joins a branch or a vase unites with the space around.

When we look to traditional musical forms, and in particular to the musical connection system, the correspondences between the modes and melodies and the system of the bazaar are striking.

The musician moves from the mode to the melodies in a particular way; there is a system of connection. Small or short melodies never leave the mode. They stay at the same scale but use a different tone. They act as dependent indoor spaces in relation to the line. However, through the use of a central melody (*shāh gūshah*), one

moves into a new area where the beginning note is called a witness (*shāhid*). This moves through an introductory phase which is the transition into the central melody or culmination space.

A composition is essentially several melodies put together following a traditional order that involves an increasingly higher range for successive melodies. The bazaar is essentially a series of dependent spaces, sometimes emphasized through a space which serves as a crossing with an elevated roof, which heightens the main line of the bazaar.

Each melody has a descent (*furūd*), a short melody played at the conclusion of a longer melody to connect it to the parent mode; as one re-enters the main bazaar space from the nodal spaces, one moves through the same descent back to the parent line.

The melody or tonal system provides the model and rhythmic features of a composition. It shapes the melody by giving it mood and character. It is the *Gestalt* of traditional music: it provides something more than the sum of the parts. The same is true of the traditional spatial system. The rhythm of dependent spaces, with the variation of openings to nodal spaces, provides a *Gestalt*.

In the tonal system the generic features of the melodies are range (location and extent of tones), configuration of notes (in the range) and the hierarchy of notes (notes of stress, stopping, etc.). In the spatial system the generic features are the range of spaces, their location and extent, their geometric configuration, and the spatial connection system which provides a hierarchy of spaces within the main order.

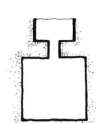

Architecture

connection

transition

culmination

Pottery

mouth

neck

body

Botany

connection

stem

leaf

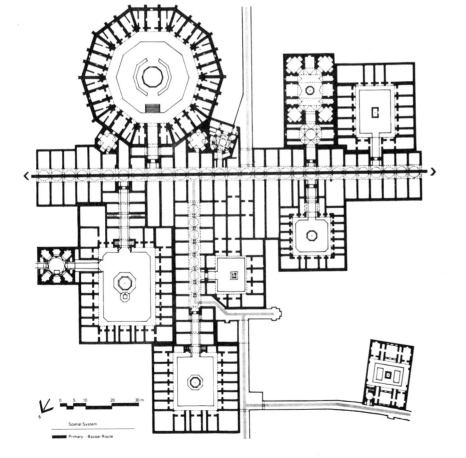

From far left:

Spatial connection system: the bazaar, Rezaiyeh, Iran.

Outdoor nodal space: the main courtyard of a *madrasah* or college, the Madrasah-yi-Nimawar, Isfahān, Iran.

Spatial system: plan of segment of the bazaar, Kāshān, Iran, by Nader Ardalan. The darker line is the primary bazaar route, the lighter the secondary residential paths; nodal spaces are outlined with broken lines.

Primary movement system, diagrams from Ardalan and Bakhtiar, *The Sense of Unity*.

Rhythm and Symmetry

Traditional architecture captures space through geometric forms. Traditional music relates to melodies (gūshah-hā) rather than scales (that is, space rather than shape) as the framework of a composition. By symmetrically repeating the forms in serial or circular order, a moving architecture is created that reads like a musical composition. Serial or binary forms balance and succeed each other in arithmetical proportion, as seen in the symmetry of the dependent spaces along the route of the bazaar.

In the ternary or circular form, the dividing line between two symmetrical halves becomes an autonomous connecting space which delays the fulfilment of the symmetry. Repetition fulfils the symmetry through a balance of total impressions. A courtyard space may balance a domed sanctuary space, the connection being the īwān or porch.

As the movement system extends, combinations of serial and circular symmetry become apparent. Dependent spaces of various sizes repeat themselves (a, b, c, d, a); or alternating dependent and nodal spaces combine binary and ternary or serial and circular symmetrical forms (a, b, a, b, a). Each of the dependent or nodal spaces is itself designed according to geometrical laws, and their symmetrical repetition constitutes the flow.

The role of time in traditional architecture lies in rhythm, the succession of boundary lines that allow an unbroken rhythmic flow, like the waves of the sea: 'Macrocosmically and microcosmically, nature has disposed itself in rhythm. Only through rhythm is one able to escape the prison of time. Nature contains continual repetition, inspiring man to imitate her in her mode of operation through an open-ended, continuous movement system.' (Ardalan and Bakhtiar, *The Sense of Unity*.)

Circular and serial symmetry: plan of segment of the bazaar, Kāshān, Iran, from Ardalan and Bakhtiar, *The Sense of Unity*. The lettering denotes the individuality of each unit along the main bazaar route (see previous page).

Serial symmetry:

a, a, a, a, . . . a
→

Circular symmetry, tertiary:

1	2	3	4	5	6	7	8
aba	aca	ada	efe	aga	hih	aja	aka

Circular symmetry, binary:

9
hh

Combined circular and serial patterns:

(i) The tempo and therefore the musical (spatial) character of this particular 'movement' is created by the cumulative serial and circular rhythms encountered there in motion. Thus:

   2   4   5   7   8

. . . a a a a a a a a c a a a a e f e a g a a a a j a a a a k a a a a . . .

a a a a a a b a a a a d a a a a a a a a h h i h h a a a a a a a a . . .

   1   3   6

(ii) A 'movement' (such as the coppersmiths' bazaar) constitutes one of many within the total open-ended composition of a bazaar (see iii):

. . . a a a a a/a a a a a a a a e f e a g a a a j a a a a k a/a a . . .

. . . a a a a a/a b a a a a d a a a a a a a a h h i h h a a a a a/a a . . .

interval   movement I (coppersmiths' bazaar)   interval

(iii) Movements within the composition of a bazaar:

interval .	movement I	. interval .	movement II	. interval .	movement III	interval	movement IV .
	coppersmiths' bazaar		tanners' bazaar		shoemakers' bazaar		woodworkers' bazaar

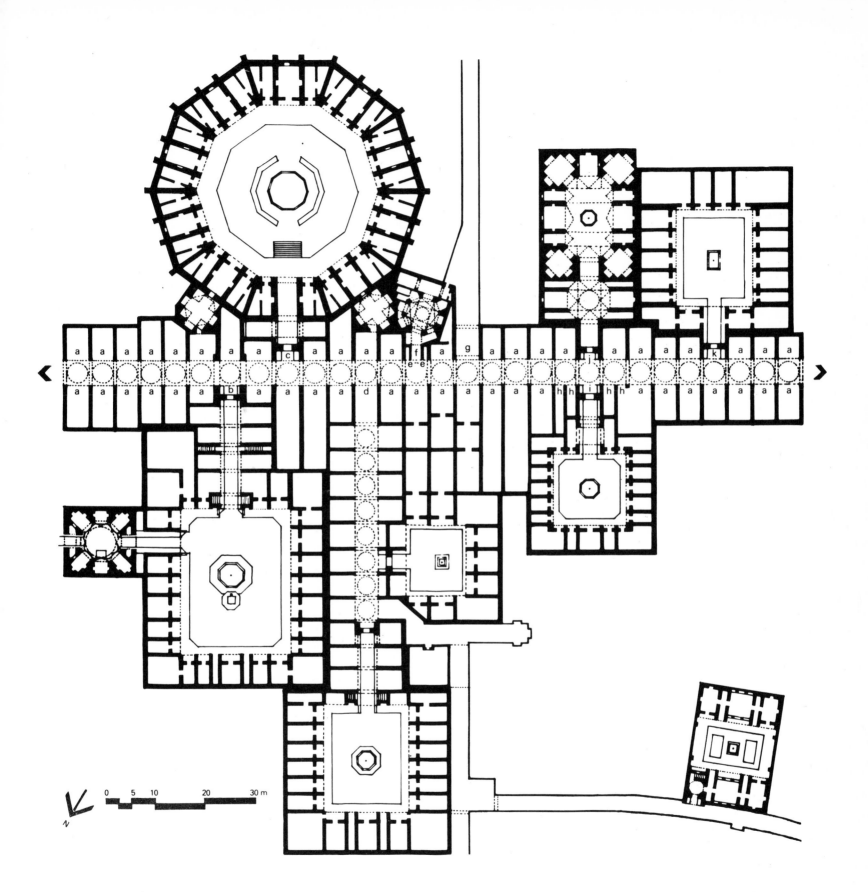

MYSTICAL POETRY

Mystical poetry may be described as a harmony of religion, philosophy and art, constituting the deepest and finest expression of the mystic spirit. It is a synthesis of thought, feeling and imagination which recalls and awakens the inner senses.

Arabic was the first language in which Sufis, whatever their nationality, were accustomed to teach and write. The early tracts and epistles abound in technical terms and were evidently not addressed to persons untrained in theology. They form the basis for the popular and poetical form of Sufism. In the tenth century there was a flowering of literature in Persian which was to inspire most of the later Sufi poetic expression.

The Sufis first turned to the *rubāʿī* form, which made no pretensions to learning and could readily be adopted to express mystical thought and sentiment in a simple way. The *qaṣīda* and *ghazal* were also cultivated, but it was not until the *mathnawī* form was created and borrowed from epic poetry that the full powers of Sufi expression were allowed to blossom. The Sufi *mathnawī* is didactic, and appears to be modelled on its prose counterpart, the discourse or sermon preached by a Shaykh to the disciples who gathered around him. This form accepts

legends from the Quran, traditions of the Prophet, sayings, anecdotes, and miracles of holy men, parables, allegories and so forth. Whether the *mathnawī* is a general survey of Sufi doctrine or a romance depicting the soul's love for God and her pilgrimage in Quest of Him, as a rule it introduces many other stories.

The combination of six elements determined by whether the word has two (1st mobile, 2nd quiet), two (both mobile), three (1st and 2nd mobile, 3rd quiet), three (1st and 3rd mobile, 2nd quiet) four (1st three mobile, 4th quiet) or five (1st four mobile, 5th quiet) letters gives rise to seven principal feet. Persian metric notation is through long (l) and short (o) sounds.

Starting with the principle that Persian poetry has four tempos, formed from a certain number of measures all of which are reducible to eight short beats including rests, the quaver or eighth note is the unit of measure used to show the relationship of music to metre.

The union of two or more feet gives rise to a metre. A half-verse is called a hemistich. A group of two verses, or quatrain, is called a *rubāʿī*. In this form, the first, second and fourth hemistichs must rhyme among themselves. Some poets

even make the four hemistichs rhyme together. A group of 6 to 13 verses is called a *ghazal* or ode. The form of the ode is used primarily for love poems, which often veil mystic intuitions. The two hemistichs of the first verse should rhyme, and thereafter only the second hemistichs of the verses rhyme together.

If the number of verses exceeds fifteen we have a *qaṣīdah*, in which the two hemistichs of the first verse must be equal in letters and movement. The *mathnawī* is a form in which each verse has a particular rhyme and each pair of hemistichs rhymes together. The second chart shows the metres of some works of poetry and their musical transcription.

The care given to the details of each verse of poetry, within the poem as a totality unified by a single rhyme and dominated by one general sentiment, is a structural principle which appears in all Sufi arts. Each verse corresponds to the primary image of the arabesque in its continued repetition of a single theme.

All the metaphysical, cosmological, psychological and religious symbols described in this book (see pp. 25–30, 56–63) can be found in mystical poetry. But there are certain symbols which remain part of one particular means of expression, and this holds true for mystical poetry as well as for other art forms.

Although the mystical poets all relate to the Islamic tradition in seeking the inward spiritual journey, they often find themselves in disagreement with exotericists who follow the Divine Law but refuse to allow that the inner spiritual journey is possible. Symbols evolved which shocked the general public, and it was for this reason that many of the poets were felt to be heretics. In fact, they are expressing a subtle point by using words from the Quran in a special way. While outwardly defying the jurists, they inwardly embodied in their work the Way of Islam.

It should be pointed out that these poetic images are not simply metaphors, if we define metaphor in the Aristotelian sense of 'a transference based on the observation of analogy'. It is not the case that an extraordinary experience occurs to a mystic and then the mystic describes it through a metaphor. On the contrary, the

Musical Transcription	English Transliteration	Persian Transcription	Feet
♪₁ ♪ ♪ ♩. ɣ ₁	FAʿūLoN	۱ه۱ه۰	فَعولُن
₁♪. ♪ ♪ ɣ ₁	FAʿeLoN	۱ه۰ه۰	فَاعِلُن
♪ ₁ ♪ ♪♪♪. ɣ ₁	MaFAʿiLoN	۱ه۱ه۱ه۰۰	مَفاعِیلُن
♪₁ ♪. ♪ ♪ ɣ ₁	MoSTafʿaLoN	۱ه۰ه۱ه	مُستفعِلُن
₁♪. ♪ ♪ ♪₁	FAʿeLaToN	۱ه۱ه۰ه۱ه	فَاعِلاتُن
♪₁ ♪. ♪ ♪. ɣ ₁	MoFAʿeLaToN	۱ه۰۰ه۰۰	مُفاعِلَتُن
♪₁ ♪. ♪ ♪. ɣ ₁	MoTeFAʿeLoN	۱ه۰۱ه۰۰۰	مُتَفاعِلُن

vision or image *is* the metaphor, and this is why the terms we are about to describe are really symbols, for the expressions used by the mystics are simply the sensible form in which the mystic sees Reality.

A world of metaphorical experiences was expressed in poetry through images drawn from pre-Islamic traditions: wine, the cup-bearer, the tavern and intoxicants, all of which are forbidden in the Quran in their outward form. Sufi poets took these words and through spiritual hermeneutics interpreted them at a metaphysical-psychological level.

Wine is a symbol for the ecstasy which causes the Sufi to be beside himself when in the presence of a vision or emanation of the Beloved. It is the symbol of the Absolute, manifested and present. Wine is the catalyst which causes a motion between the mystic's soul and the spiritual vision; and for the mystic this is love, which is itself the goal of the Quest, and yet, paradoxically, forms the greatest obstacle to the seeker.

The cup-bearer, *sāqī*, causes one to drink; and it is the attention of the *sāqī* that one seeks. The cup-bearer brings the wine of love and affection, and symbolizes the Shaykh who guides one through love to drink of Divine Knowledge.

The tavern, *may khāneh*, symbolizes the heart of the mystic, the dwelling-place of love, love which expands the traveller's heart. The wine-seller or vintner, *khammar*, is the perfect disciple who knows the Qualities of God and the essence of Muḥammad (ﷺ). To be a 'haunter of taverns' is to be freed of self: for the tavern is in a world that has no similitude. The tavern is a sanctuary which has no place; it is the nest of the bird of the soul.

Intoxicated ones, *mastān*, are lovers of God, Sufis who are drowned in the sea of Unity, acquainted with mysteries but unaware of the vicissitudes of this world. They are ones who have a vision of the Beloved which has no semblance to the sensible world of existence.

The veil symbolizes another aspect of self to the mystic poet. Veils are feelings of guilt, so to be veiled is to be ashamed because of sin. When the mystic attaches self to the Shaykh, the Friend of God he sells his veiledness, his shamedness, and comes closer to the Divine.

Poet	Work	Musical transcription	Metre
Nizami	*Laylā and Majnun*	*(musical notation)*	مفعول مفاعلن فعولن مفعول مفاعلن فعولن
Nizami	*Treasury of Mysteries*	*(musical notation)*	مفتعلن مفتعلن فاعلات مفتعلن مفتعلن فاعلات
Firdawsi Nizami Sa'di	*Shah-Nāmeh* *Iskandar-Nāmeh* *Boustān*	*(musical notation)*	فعولن فعولن فعولن فعول فعولن فعولن فعولن فعول
Rūmī Aṭṭār	*Mathnawī* *Conference of the Birds*	*(musical notation)*	فاعلاتن فاعلاتن فاعلات فاعلاتن فاعلاتن فاعلات
Sanai Nizami Amir Khosroe	*Enclosed Garden of Truth* *Seven Portraits* *Eight Paradises*	*(musical notation)*	فاعلاتن مفاعلن فعولن فاعلاتن مفاعلن فعولن
Jami Nizami Khaqani Pahlavi	*Yūsūf and Zulaykha* *Khosroe and Shīrīn* *History of the Gnostics* *Pahlaviat*	*(musical notation)*	مفاعيلن مفاعيلن فعولن مفاعيلن مفاعيلن فعولن
Jami Amir Khosroe	*Rosary of the Pious* *Nine Heavens*	*(musical notation)*	فاعلاتن فعلاتن فعلن فاعلاتن فعلاتن فعلن

Musical transcriptions, names and traditional notation of the seven principal feet in Persian poetry.

Musical transcription of the metres of sixteen major works of Persian poetry.

THE SCIENCE OF LETTERS
Ilm-i-abjad

The concept that the nature and secret of a letter is alive when it is compounded to form words, while words are correspondingly alive within created things, is the basic principle of the science of letters. All created things move in different stages because of the constant renewal of creation; and the secret of all created things lies in the word. The Sufi authors of treatises on the science of letters affirm that this science reveals the beautiful Names of God as manifested in the world of nature. These Divine expressions originate in the letters which hold the secrets alive within created things.

Some Sufis considered the secret was in the inherent temperament of a letter. They divided the letters into four groups, symbolizing the four elements through their inherent nature. Thus,

fiery letters repel cold diseases, and increase heat when it is desirable in both its physical and astrological sense. Watery letters repel hot diseases, such as fevers, and increase cold powers.

Still others relate that the secret lies in the letters' relation to numerical proportion. Letters of the alphabet indicate numerical values, which by nature are inherent in them. Thus there comes to exist a correspondence between letters and their numerical value. For instance, there is a relationship between b (ب), k (ک), and r (ر), because all three of them indicate 2 in its different positions.

There are magic squares for words as well as for numbers. Each group of letters has its numerical value, and thus a particular kind of magic square which fits it.

Fire	أ	ه	ط	م	ف	س/ش	ذ
	1	5	9	40	80	300	700
Air	ب	و	ى	ن	ض/ص	ت	ظ/ض
	2	6	10	50	90	400	800
Water	ج	ز	ک	ص/س	ق	ث	غ/ظ
	3	7	20	60	100	500	900
Earth	د	ح	ل	ع	ر	خ	ش/غ
	4	8	30	70	200	600	1000

West/East

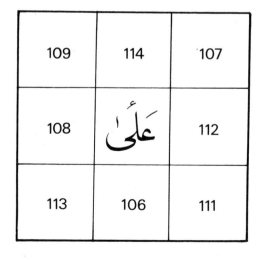

109	114	107
108	علّی	112
113	106	111

فتلقى	آدم	من	ربه	كلمات	فتاب
آدم	من	ربه	كلمات	فتاب	عليه
من	ربه	كلمات	فتاب	عليه	انه
ربه	كلمات	فتاب	عليه	انه	هو
كلمات	فتاب	عليه	انه	هو	التواب
فتاب	عليه	انه	هو	التواب	الرحيم

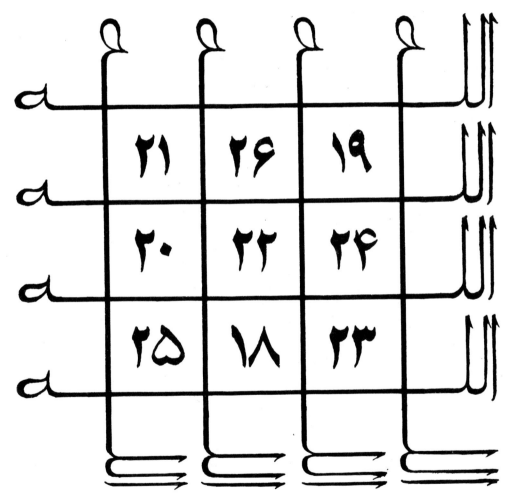

From far left:

Letters were divided according to their correspondences with the four elements, and a number was attached to each of them. The systems differed between the eastern and western ends of the Islamic world.

The numerical significance of the Divine Name 'Alī, 'the Almighty', from which was derived the name of the son-in-law of the Prophet, can be determined by adding up the numbers in any complete row and subtracting the two numbers left and right of (or above and below) centre.

Verse 37 of chapter 2 of the Quran, 'thereafter Adam received certain words from his Lord, and He turned towards him', is above distributed so that it can be read in a number of ways.

The Divine Name *Allāh* corresponds to 66. Left, the square itself is formed of the Name, containing thrice three numbers which in any direction add up to 66:

21	26	19
20	22	24
25	18	23

MYSTICAL DREAMS
Ruya'ha

The mystical dream in Sufism is a spiritual ethos that is found within the prophetic traditions of Islam. As Muḥammad is the last Prophet in our cycle of humanity, the Sufi is never in doubt that the dreams and visions which he personally receives testify to his Saintship (*walāyat*) and not to Prophethood (*nubuwwat*). Mystical dreams are, in other words, expressions of inspiration, not of revelation; for the concept of *walāyat* relates to the spiritual initiation of the 'people of God'.

The gesture of mystical dreams points to the *'ālam-i-mithāl*, the world of symbols and similitudes, the *mundus imaginalis*. This world exists between the sensible, phenomenal world and the world of intelligible noumena:

'The *mundus imaginalis* is a world of autonomous forms and images, forms in suspense, that is, not inherent in a material substratum like the colour black in a black table, but 'in suspense' in the place of their appearance, in the imagination, like an image suspended in a mirror. It is a perfectly real world, preserving all the richness and diversity of the sensible world but in a spiritual state. The existence of this world presupposes that it is possible to leave the sensible state without leaving physical extension . . . Neither the physical senses nor the pure intellect are the organs apprehending this world; it is grasped by 'suprasensible senses', essentially an imaginative consciousness. . . . It is not fantasy.

We must posit that "the imagination is the incarnation of thought in image and the placing of the image *in being*".' (H. Corbin, 'The Visionary Dream in Islamic Spirituality'.)

According to Mulla Ṣadrā, the sixteenth-century Persian theosopher, 'the active imagination is like the Intellect, a purely spiritual faculty whose existence is not conditioned by the physical organism'.

This theory of imaginative knowledge, thought activated by imagination, forms the basis for the validity of suprasensible perceptions and mystical dreams.

The mystic, in exile, prays ceaselessly from the depth of being to be given a friend, a teacher of truth, a companion and spiritual guide to lead the Way. For the whole meaning of existence to the Sufi is to find the Way of the return. It cannot be accomplished without a guide. What is essential is the individual, personal bond between the initiate and the initiator. The initiator appears under various names: 'Perfect Nature', 'the witness in Heaven', 'the angel of the philosopher', 'the invisible master', and so forth; but the concept is always one of an archetypical level where one encounters one's inner spiritual guide.

Expressions of mystical visions and dreams which were spiritual initiations for the Sufi abound and no more than a few can be shown here.

Fantasy on marbled paper, Turkish school, 16th c., by courtesy of the Fogg Art Museum, Harvard University (Purchase – Grace Nichols Strong Fund, Francis H. Burr Fund, and Friends of the Fogg Art Museum Fund).

Rūzbehān Baqlī of Shīrāz (d. 1209)

I seemed to be in my vision on the mountain of the east, and I saw there a great group of angels. From the east to the west stretched a vast sea. There was nothing else to be seen. Then the angels said to me, 'Enter the sea and swim to the west.' I entered the sea and began to swim. When I arrived at the place of the setting sun as it was going down, I saw a group of angels on the mountain of the west; they were illuminated by the light of the setting sun. They called to me, 'You, down below, swim and have no fear.' When I at last reached the mountain, they said to me, 'No one has crossed this sea except ʿAlī ibn Abī Ṭālib and you after him.'

Muḥyiʾd Dīn Ibn ʿArabī (d. 1240)

The power of the active imagination develops in me to the point that it presents my mystic beloved to me visually in a bodily, objective, extra-mental figure just as the Angel Gabriel appeared bodily to the eyes of the Prophet. At first, I did not feel strong enough to look at this figure. It spoke to me. I heard and understood. These apparitions left me in such a state that for many days I could not take any nourishment. Each time I went to the table, the figure was standing at the table's end, looking at me and saying in a language I could hear with my ears: 'Will you eat while contemplating me?' It was impossible for me to eat, but I did not feel hunger! I was so full of my vision that I stuffed myself and became drunken in contemplating the figure to the point that this contemplation took the place of all nourishment. My good appearance astonished my friends who knew of my total abstinence. The fact is that I continued for a long time without tasting a bit of food, not experiencing either hunger or thirst. All the while this figure was never out of my sight whether I was standing or sitting, moving or resting.

Najmoddīn Kobrā (d. 1221)

When the circle of the face has become pure, it gives off light like a spring emptying water, so that the mystic has a feeling (by his awareness of the suprasensible) of flashing lights irradiating from his face. This flashing appears between the eyes and the eyebrows. It continues until it covers the whole face. When this happens, there appears before you, facing your face, another Face, equally of light. It also radiates light, while behind its transparent veil a sun becomes visible which appears to be animated by oscillation. Actually this Face is your own face, and the sun is the sun of the Spirit who comes and goes in your body. Later, purity submerges all your person, and behold you see before you a person of light from which lights also irradiate. The mystic notices these lights proceeding from his entire person. Often the veil falls revealing the whole reality of the person, and it is then that you perceive all with the whole of your body. The opening of interior vision, the vision's organ of light, begins with the eyes, continues to the face, followed by the breast, finally by the entire body. It is this person of light before you who is called the suprasensible guide in Sufic terminology.

Shamsoddīn Lāhījī (d. 1506)

One night after prayers were finished and the liturgical recitation prescribed for the nocturnal hours, I continued to meditate. Absorbed in ecstasy, I had a vision. There was a khānaqah extremely lofty. It was open, and I was inside the khānaqah. Suddenly, I saw that I was outside. I saw that the entire universe, in the structure it presents, consists of light. Everything had become one colour, and all the atoms of all the beings proclaimed, 'I am the Truth,' each in the manner proper to its being and with the force particular to each. I was unable to interpret properly what manner of being had made them proclaim this. Having seen these things in my vision, an intoxication and an exaltation, a desire and an extraordinary delectation were born within me. I wanted to fly in the air, but I saw that there was something resembling a piece of wood at my feet which prevented my taking flight. With violent emotion, I kicked the ground in every possible manner until this piece of wood let go. Like an arrow shooting forth from the bow, but a hundred times stronger, I rose and moved into the distance. When I arrived at the first Heaven, I saw that the moon had split, and I passed through the moon. Then returning from this state and absence, I found myself again present.

COSMOLOGY AND SPIRITUAL ASTRONOMY

Sufi cosmology is based on Alexandrian hermeticism, and its spontaneous identification of appearances, constant and rhythmic, of the sensible world with its eternal prototypes.

Ibn 'Arabī encompasses the essential truth of a heliocentric universe in his cosmology. The sun is the pole (qutb) and the heart of the world. It has a central position in the hierarchy of the celestial spheres: there are seven spheres above the sun and seven below it. The Divine Throne symbolizes the synthesis of all of the cosmos, and at the opposite end is the earth, the centre of fixation.

The Zā'irajah is a table, devised by as-Sabtī, in which, through astrology and the science of letters, one is able to answer questions about the future. The procedure is very complicated, and only a brief summary can be given here.

The operation with a question requires seven principles: (1) the number of the letters of the chord; (2) the retention of their cycles after division by twelve; (3) the knowledge of the degree of the ascendant; (4) the ruler of the zodiacal sign; (5) the greatest principal cycle which is always one; (6) the result of adding the ascendant to the principal cycle; and (7) the result of multiplying ascendant plus cycle by the ruler of the zodiacal sign and of adding the ruler of the sign to the ascendant. The whole operation takes place in three cycles multiplied by four.

Ibn 'Arabī describes the setting out of the universe through correspondences which relate the macrocosm to the microcosm: 'God set the sun to be a lamp to give light to the people of the earth (71:15–16), and likewise He has set the Spirit [rūḥ] in the body to give light to the body thereby, so that when it departs at death, the body is darkened, just as the earth is darkened when the sun disappears. Then He set the Intellect ['aql] to be as the moon which shines in the heavenly vault, at one time waxing and at another waning. At its beginning it is small, being the new moon, just as the intelligence is but small when man is little, but increases like as the moon increases to the night of its fullness, after which it begins to decrease. . . . Then He placed in the sky the five stars [Mercury, Venus, Jupiter, Mars and Saturn], namely, the stars of retrograde motion which run backwards, to which correspond the five senses, i.e. taste, smell, touch, hearing and seeing.

'Then in the world of the heavens He set a Throne and a Pedestal. The Throne He brought into existence and set as something to which the hearts of His servants might turn, a place to which they might raise their hands, not as a place where He Himself might be or as a symbol of His Qualities, for in the case of the Merciful One – exalted be He – the sitting is but one of the qualifying, descriptive epithets applied to Him. These qualifying, descriptive epithets are connected with His essence, whereas the Throne is one of the things He created. It is not attached to Him, does not touch Him, He is not borne by it, and He has no need of it. As for the Pedestal, it is the storehouse of His secrets, the quiver for holding His lights; and the heavens and the earth are the depository for all that is in the circle of His wide-spreading Pedestal. So He has set man's breast to be as the Pedestal, for in it are stored all the attainments of knowledge. It stands like a courtyard at the gate of the heart and the soul, with two doors opening to them, so that all good proceeding from the heart or evil proceeding from the soul is stored in the breast from which it proceeds to the productive members.

'The heart He set to be as the Throne. His Throne in the heavens is something known about, whereas His throne on earth is a lodging-place, and thus the throne of the heart is a nobler thing than the Throne of the heavens, for that Throne is not wide enough for Him; does not bear Him; does not perceive Him; but this throne is something towards which at all times He looks, to which He reveals Himself, or to which He sends down from heaven His bounty, for He has said: "My heavens were not wide enough to hold Me, nor My earth, but the heart of my believing servant holds Me".' (Ibn 'Arabī, Shajarat-al-kawn.)

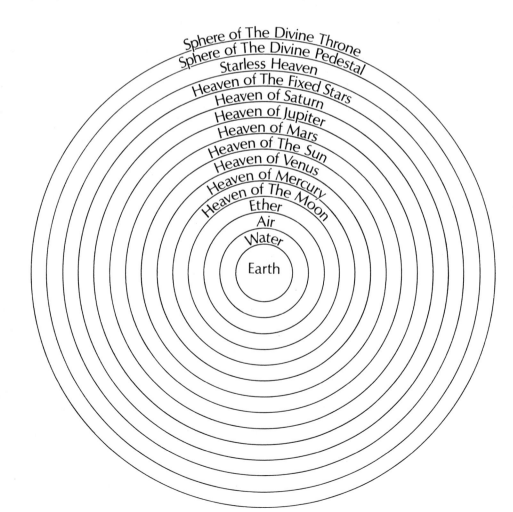

The celestial spheres in the cosmology of Ibn 'Arabī.

The Zā'irajah of as-Sabtī, diagram by Liam Dunne from Ibn Khaldūn, The Muqaddimah.

The diagram labels, from outer to inner:
Sphere of The Divine Throne
Sphere of The Divine Pedestal
Starless Heaven
Heaven of The Fixed Stars
Heaven of Saturn
Heaven of Jupiter
Heaven of Mars
Heaven of The Sun
Heaven of Venus
Heaven of Mercury
Heaven of The Moon
Ether
Air
Water
Earth

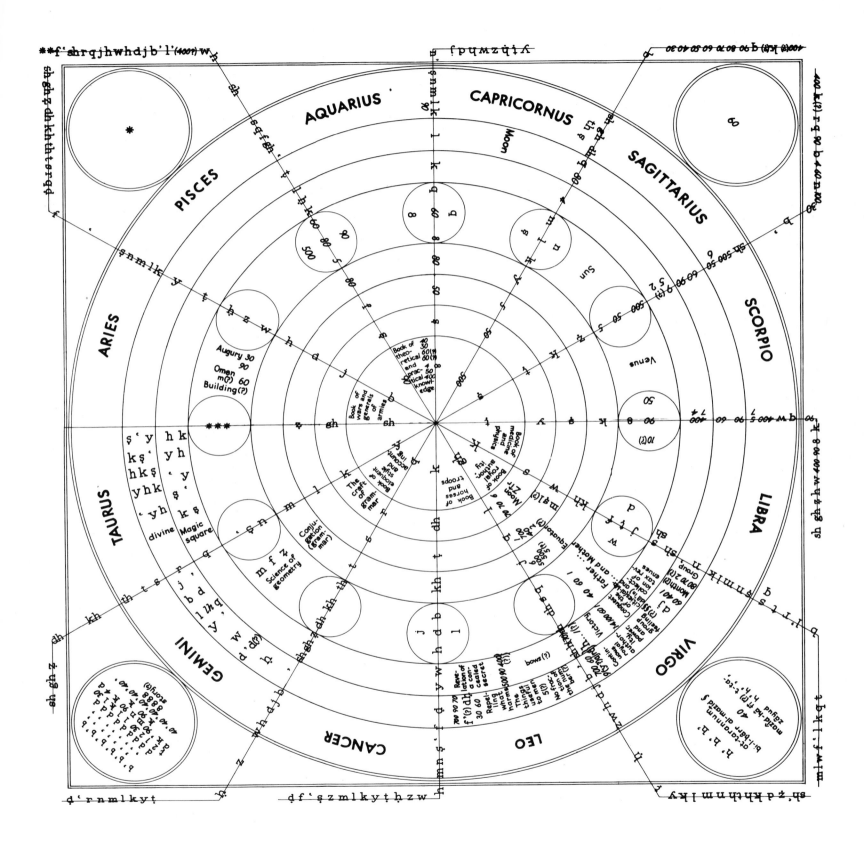

Sources and Further Reading

Anṣārī al-Harawī, ʿAbd Allāh. *Les Étapes des itinérants vers Dieu*, trans. S. de Laugier de Beaurecueil O.P., Paris 1962.

Ardalan, Nader, and Laleh Bakhtiar. *The Sense of Unity: The Sufi Tradition in Persian Architecture*, Chicago 1971.

Arberry, A. J. *The Koran Interpreted*, 2 vols, London and New York 1964.

Aṭṭār, Farid al-Din. *The Conference of the Birds*, trans. C. S. Nott, London 1969.

Browne, E. G. *A Literary History of Persia*, 4 vols, Cambridge 1964.

Burckhardt, Titus. *Alchemy*, trans. William Stoddart, London 1967.

———. *Clé spirituelle de l'astrologie musulmane d'après Mohyiddin Ibn ʿArabī*, Paris 1950.

———. *Sacred Art East and West*, London 1967.

Corbin, Henry. *Avicenna and the Visionary Recitals*, trans. Willard R. Trask, New York 1960 and London 1961.

———. *Creative Imagination in the Sufism of Ibn ʿArabī*, trans. Ralph Manheim, Princeton and London 1969.

———. 'Physiologie de l'Homme de lumière dans le Soufisme iranien', in *Ombre et lumière*, Paris 1961.

———. 'The Visionary Dream in Islamic Spirituality', in *Dreams and Society*, ed. G. E. Von Gruenbaum, Los Angeles 1964.

al-Ghazālī, Majd Dīn al-Ṭūsī. *Tracts on Listening to Music*, trans. James Robson, London 1938.

Guyard, S. *La Théorie nouvelle de la métrique arabe*, Paris 1940.

Ibn ʿArabī. *Shajarat-al-kawn*, trans. Arthur Jeffrey, *Journal of the Royal Asiatic Society*, 1959, pp. 119–21.

Ibn Khaldūn, *The Muqaddimah*, trans. Franz Rosenthal, New York 1958.

Izutsu, Toshihiko. *The Key Philosophical Concepts in Sufism and Taoism – Ibn ʿArabī and Lao-Tzu, Chuang-Tzu*, Tokyo 1966.

Lings, Martin. *A Sufi Saint of the Twentieth Century*, London 1971.

Nasr, Seyyed Hossein. *An Introduction to Islamic Cosmological Doctrines*, Cambridge, Mass., 1964.

———. *Science and Civilization in Islam*, Cambridge, Mass. 1968.

———. *Sufi Essays*, London and Albany, N.Y., 1972.

———. *Three Muslim Sages*, Cambridge, Mass., and Oxford 1964.

Nicholson, Reynold. *Studies in Islamic Mysticism*, Cambridge 1967.

Pope, Arthur Upham, and Phyllis Ackerman, eds. *A Survey of Persian Art*, 14 vols. London and New York 1965.

Rūmī, Jalāl al-Dīn. *The Mathnawī*, trans. R. A. Nicholson, London 1969.

Sirāj al-Dīn, Abū Bakr. *The Book of Certainty*, London 1952.

Schuon, Frithjof. *Dimensions of Islam*, trans. Peter Townsend, London 1969.

———. *Stations of Wisdom*, trans. G. E. H. Palmer, London and Toronto 1961.

Shabistarī, Maḥmūd. *Gulshan-i-rāz (The Garden of Mystery)*, trans. E. H. Whinfield, London 1880.

Zonis, Ella. *Classical Persian Music*, Cambridge, Mass. 1973.

Zuckerkandl, Victor. *Sound and Symbol*, Princeton 1969.

Acknowledgments

I wish to express my gratitude to Nader Ardalan, Seyyed Hossein Nasr, Jamshid Bakhtiar, Peter Wilson and William Chittick *for reading and commenting upon the manuscript; and to* Shireen Bakhtiar Javid, Karl Schlamminger, Keith Critchlow, Gholam Reza Amirzadeh, Beijan Ellahi and Ali Afshar *for helping with the illustrations.*

Objects in the plates, pp. 33–92, are in the collections of the author 60, 68, 74; Cambridge, Mass. Fogg Art Museum, Harvard University, Gift N. 63; Dublin, Chester Beatty Library and Gallery of Oriental Art 52, 81, 83; Istanbul, Museum of Turkish and Islamic Art 56; Lisbon, Gulbenkian Foundation 77; London, British Museum 80, 87; New York, Metropolitan Museum of Art Fletcher Fund, 1963 36, Collection of Arthur A. Houghton 37, Gift of Arthur A. Houghton, Jr., 1970 44; Rogers Fund, 1910 57; 80; New York, Pierpont Morgan Library 84; New York, Public Library, Spencer Collection 45; Oxford, Bodleian Library 70; Paris, Bibliothèque Nationale 89; Jalil Rassouli 39, 54, 55; Mr and Mrs Karl Schlamminger 38, 40, 75; Tehran, Museum of Decorative Arts 76; Tehran, Gulistan Museum 69; Uppsala, University Library 66, 67.

Photographs were supplied by Nader Ardalan 33, 42, 47, 48, 49, 58, 86, 91, 92, 93–4 (not Konya), 102, 107, 109; Yolande Crowe 79; His Excellency Mr James George 71; Knightsbridge Carpet Galleries 50; Wim Swaan (from Rom Landau, *Morocco*, published by Paul Elek Productions Ltd, London 1967) 59; Turkish Ministry of Tourism 41, 53, 72, 94 (Konya); Roger Wood 43, 51, 61, 73, 108.